when a child dies

Stories of Survival and Hope

edited by RICHARD S. HIPPS

SMYTH&HELWYS
PUBLISHING, INCORPORATED   MACON, GEORGIA

Smyth & Helwys Publishing, Inc.
6316 Peake Road
Macon, Georgia 31210-3960
1-800-747-3016
© 1996, 2001 by Smyth & Helwys Publishing
All rights reserved.
Printed in the United States of America.

Richard S. Hipps, editor

The paper used in this publication meets the minimum
requirements of American National Standard for Information
Sciences—Permanence of Paper for Printed Library Materials.
ANSI Z39.48–1984   (alk. paper)

Library of Congress Cataloging-in-Publication Data

When a child dies: stories of survival and hope/
edited by Richard S. Hipps
p. cm.
ISBN 1-57312-032-4
1. Children—Death—Religious aspects—Christianity
2. Grief—Religious aspects—Christianity
3. Bereavement—Religious aspects—Christianity
I. Hipps, Richard S.

BV4907.L57 1996
248.8'6—dc20

95-48116
CIP

CONTENTS

To the Memory of
Bethany
Laura Lue
Philip
Alex
Matthew
Bryan
Janet
Susan
Roger
Don

I heard a voice from heaven saying, "Write this: Blessed are the dead who from now on die in the Lord." "Yes," says the Spirit, "they will rest from their labors, for their deeds follow them."

(Rev 14:13)

PREFACE

In one of his plays, Tennessee Williams tells about a mentally disturbed woman who is sitting at a card table in her garden. She is desperately trying to work a jigsaw puzzle. She is extremely tense. Her hands are shaking as she tries to force the pieces together that will not fit. Some of the pieces fall off the table. The woman becomes more and more frustrated. Finally, she looks at her daughter and says poignantly, "The pieces don't fit together! The pieces don't fit together!"

That's the way it is for those of us who have lost children. The pieces don't fit together and perhaps never will. We cling to our faith, pick up the pieces, and make the most of what life has left for us.

This book was written by grieving parents to help with the practical questions, emotional afflictions, and spiritual challenges involved in the death of a child. If you are wondering what kind of future you could have following a similar personal tragedy, you are likely to find new hope in what you are about to read.

The way our children died is discussed in detail. Our lives have been changed forever by AIDS, cancer, heart disease, polio, drunk drivers, a tornado ripping through a house, and a motor bike accident. Some persons write out of the context of recent loss, while others write from the perspective of forty years of grieving.

For those who have lost a child, reading our stories will help you better appreciate the fact that you are not alone with your thoughts and feelings. Stories are powerful. Stories hold our world together. They connect us. Without stories we remain isolated and vulnerable.

Let this book open your heart. It is not only for those who are perplexed about the mystery of their misery; it is also for those who are concerned about the trials and tribulations of others. But to you, bereaved parent, we offer our love and understanding. We've been there.

ACKNOWLEDGMENTS

Producing a book such as this one is a collective effort. I want to express my deep appreciation to all of the contributors who made this book possible. Their stories reveal the determination of the Christian spirit when it refuses to be broken by adversity.

The contributions of Joan and Jean Bennett to this book are immeasurable. Their intelligence and sensitivity command my total admiration and gratitude. I will always remember what their mama told them when she was living through her darkest days: "I'm going to live in hope . . . even if I die in despair."

Every pastor needs two secretaries like Myrtle Kelly and LaDelle Kay. I thank them for always being there when I needed them. Finally, I wish to thank my wife, Patricia, who is an enduring source of inspiration for me and a wonderful person with whom to spend the rest of my life. I also thank her for sharing with me the lives of our three precious children: Justin, Lacey, and Alexandra.

CHAPTER I

❧ Hope Springs Eternal ❧

Tony W. Cartledge

1 Peter 1:3; Psalm 42:5

A Brutal Teacher

The morning dawned much as any other wintry day, and there was nothing unusual to set January 18, 1994, apart from any other space in time. It was cold when the sun came up, and it stayed cold. I was in the little town of Lincolnton, Georgia, where my parents live, and where our seven-year-old daughter, Bethany, had been visiting. Bethany's school has a year-round schedule, and her track was on break for most of January. Bethany had been visiting with her Mama Hollie and Daddy Bill for a whole week, and she had a wonderful time. I had come to bring her back home, and I think she was ready.

Bethany cuddled in my lap all of Monday evening after I arrived, and on Tuesday morning early she called Jan to tell her we were on our way home and to blow her a kiss and say, "I love you, Mommy!" Together we drove for some three hours, while singing silly songs and dreaming aloud about future vacations and playing all the traveling games that keep children occupied. Bethany wanted to listen to a cassette tape that Jan had recorded, and we did. She always liked to hear her mommy sing.

We were headed north on U.S. 1 near McBee, South Carolina. The road there cuts through a forest of long-leaf pines managed by the U.S. Forest Service. Jan's tape had just ended, and Bethany was talking about the fried chicken she wanted for lunch. As we topped a long hill and came to a left-hand curve in the road, I suddenly realized that a black pickup truck was speeding toward us, *in our lane*. In the fraction of a second I had to respond, I saw him running off the road on my side, and then I veered to the left to avoid him. The strategy was good, but running off the road shook the truck driver into some sense of alertness. Suddenly and unpredictably, he jerked his truck back into the road and rammed it full speed into Bethany's door.

I remember an explosive noise, a momentary sense of violent movement, and then blackness. I don't think Bethany had a chance to remember anything, or even to know what had hit her. I hope not. In the twinkling of an eye, in the space of a single heartbeat, our bright-eyed daughter was dead. Her neck was broken, her skull was crushed, and our lives were changed forever.

When I regained some measure of consciousness, I soon realized that I had severe injuries of my own, but none of that seemed to matter when I painfully twisted around and looked into the transfixed face of my little girl. She was no longer breathing. I could not find a pulse in her neck. I could not awaken her. From the deepest part of my heart a cry escaped: *"Oh God—Bethany! Oh God—Bethany! Oh God—Bethany!"* My own cries of pain and loss soon gave way to another horrifying thought. Someone had to tell Jan that her only daughter had been killed by a drunken driver on a lonely South Carolina highway.

Lessons of the Heart

There are no adequate words to describe what an experience like this entails, or even to explain how one survives the trauma of losing a precious child so suddenly. I can tell you that our hope in God and the ministry of the members of Woodhaven Baptist Church have been vital. These have enabled us to begin the long journey toward healing and to be good stewards of our pain.

On the first Sunday I was able to return to the pulpit, I shared with our congregation three "lessons of the heart" that I had begun to learn from this awful time in our lives. First, I have learned from experience something of the absolute and terminal ugliness of sin. When I read Romans 6:23 now, it takes on new meaning. "The wages of sin is death" does not apply to the sinner alone.

Secondly, I have learned something about the importance of human choices. Because of one man's arrogant and reckless choice about his use of alcohol and his ability to drive, our daughter is dead, and there is nothing we can do to bring her back. Every decision we make has consequences, and we would do well to learn that lesson thoroughly and to remember it when we make our own choices.

Finally, I have learned—not in my head, where it already was, but in my heart—something about the centrality of our Christian hope. Let me say more about what I mean by "hope" and why I think this central tenet of faith and life is so important.

Hope for the Journey

Peter said that God, by God's great mercy, has given to us a new birth into a living hope through the resurrection of Jesus Christ from the dead (1 Pet 1:3). This living hope has kept us going in these days of emptiness and longing and gives us courage to face the future.

At times I wondered, before I knew better, if there really was that much difference between hope and faith. Both of them seemed to involve trusting in something you cannot see; one just seemed more certain than the other. Paul once said that when all else is gone, "faith, hope, and love abide" (1 Cor 13:13). I wasn't so sure that hope deserved to be in that awesome triumvirate. It seemed to me that faith and love said it all.

Let me tell you what I am learning—at least, what I am learning to be true for me. The reason hope is so important is that, when faith falters, hope is all you have left. No one can lose a child in such a senseless fashion without experiencing a crisis of faith. Hope seems to be weaker than faith, because it is less certain; but in truth hope is stronger, because it has more staying power. In our Christian pilgrimage, hope comes before faith blossoms, and hope endures even after faith falters.

When I say, "I have faith that this is true," what I really mean is that I'm absolutely convinced of this, I have experience with this, and I believe it to be true. I have had some experience, perhaps, of God's presence, and so I can say I have faith that Christ lives in me.

Now, there are other areas of life and eternity in which I have no experience, but they are of immeasurable importance to me. Since Bethany's death, thoughts of heaven and eternity have become like that for me. Before our precious child was killed, I had never lost anyone who was especially close. I won't say that heaven was not important to me, but it's just not something I thought about a whole lot. I think about it now, even as many of you do, for you may have lost loved ones, too, and heaven is important to you.

Even as I think about eternity, I cannot help but have bushels of questions and days of doubt. Is there *really* such a place as heaven? Where is it? Is Bethany *really* there, now? What is she doing? What is she thinking? Is she still conscious of what goes on here?

Hope for the Darkness

I find that I am like the man whose beloved son was sick and who entrusted him to Jesus' healing touch. He said, "If you can do anything, please take pity on us and help us." Jesus replied "If you can? Everything is possible for him who believes." And the man replied with honesty, faith, and hope: "Lord, I believe; help me overcome my unbelief!" (from Mark 9:17-27).

What happens when we want to believe so badly that it seems our life depends on it, but our faith falters, and we still have those nagging fears and unanswered questions? This is where hope comes in and where we learn its true value and what a gift it is. I have come to believe that you cannot fully experience the meaning of hope until you reach a point at which hope is all that you have left, and you cling to it like a slender, gossamer thread, holding on for dear life with both hands because that is all you have to keep your head above the waters of abject despair.

I want more than anything to be certain that Bethany is happily inhabiting heaven now, running barefoot in the sun and playing with new friends, eating cheese pizza and fish sticks and fries, and looking forward to seeing her mommy and daddy again. There is much about eternity that the Bible only hints at. There is much that I cannot know, but oh, how I hope! And with God's help, the hope that comes through Jesus Christ will continue to be enough.

I hope, I wish, and I long for greater knowing. Some of you do, too. Don't let the presence of questions convince you that faith is absent. Keep trusting and hoping in something bigger than you are and better than this world. Once, when Frederick Buechner was reflecting on the subject of hoping and wishing, he said: "Sometimes wishing is the wings the truth comes true on. Sometimes the truth is what sets us wishing for it."[1]

The presence of hope suggests that a power is at work to create that hope and set our hearts wishing for all of the promises of God. At least one psalmist knew the power of hope. On a day of exceeding disquietude, he (or she) gave voice to an internal dialogue that speaks to those who face despair:

> Why are you cast down, O my soul, and why are you disquieted within me? Hope in God; for I shall again praise him, my help and my God. (Ps 43:5)

As you face the crises and calamities that come into your life, never stop wishing or hoping, and you may then be sure that you will never stop believing. This is the power and the glory of hope.

Note

[1] *Wishful Thinking: A Theological ABC.* (New York: Harper & Row, 1973) 96.

School Days

The bus is here,
          but you are not.
Christopher is waiting for the bus.
Nicholas is waiting.
Even Andrew is waiting this year,
          but you are not.

Your clothes are here,
and your backpack,
and your lunch box,
and your pencils,
and your crayons,
          but you are not.

Your mama is here,
and your daddy,
and your fish,
          but you are not.

Your memories are here—
Your pictures are here,
Your echoes are here,
          but you are not.

Please, dear Bethany,
if there is a way,
ask God to show us that
          you are—

just in another place,
maybe another time,
wherever it is that God is,
where students learn their final lessons,
and do their eternal homework.

                                        Tony W. Cartledge

Teddy Bear Grace

Is God any more real than this teddy bear that
    rides in my lap when I drive?

It was a thought I had one day—and I thought it worth thinking about.

My teddy bear is real. It's the last one I bought for Bethany. She liked it.

My teddy bear gives me comfort.
    It is the comfort of memories shared.
    It is the comfort of touch.
    It is the comfort of stroking and patting the same soft bear that
        Bethany loved, and in the same way I used to comfort her.

Sometimes I wonder where is the comfort of God—
    why doesn't He touch me . . .
    why doesn't He show me a vision of Bethany safe and happy . . .
    why doesn't He answer all my questions?

I wonder. But yet,
    if God were to touch me,
        could I bear His glory?
    if I saw the wonders of heaven,
        could I still find beauty on earth?
    if I had answers for every question,
        would there be any place for faith?

For now, the comfort God gives is in the embrace of His people,
    in the marvels of His world,
    in the magic hope of His future,
    and in this small gift,
            this soft and furry bit of grace,
            this little teddy bear.

Tony W. Cartledge

CHAPTER 2

❧ Laura Lue ❧

Lue Ann Claypool

"Death lies on her like an untimely frost
Upon the sweetest flower of all the field."
William Shakespeare

Laura Lue died over twenty-five years ago. She was a part of my life for only ten years, unless you want to count the nine months she was developing inside my body. The time we shared now seems like another era, but not as if it happened twenty-five years ago.

The event of Laura Lue's death occupies dramatically less of my attention now than it once did, but when I am reliving it in my memory, the pain is every bit as sharp as it was that snowy winter evening when she had to leave. Unfortunately, the pain is my only link. I have to walk over broken glass to reach her. But from the beginning I knew that to avoid the pain was to obliterate her memory, and that was an idea I could not tolerate.

Losing someone who is very important to you is like an amputation. For a time the wound bleeds, and the tissue is extremely sensitive. That acute period passes, but the limb is always missing and missed. I can think of nothing that has happened to me since January 10, 1970, that would not have been improved by Laura Lue's presence. Perhaps that is why people often say about a loss that "you never get over it."

One reason the death of a child is particularly poignant is that it is unnatural. We do not articulate the expectation, but in some primordial thought pattern or instinct, we expect that our children will bury us, not we them. The death of a child is also universally mourned, by family and even by strangers, because the promise of possibility that a young life represents is unrealized. I feel almost like a guilty hoarder of the secrets of Laura Lue's charm and intelligence, that of which only a few were aware. And she remains frozen in time at age ten. The enormous energy and self-discipline that would have enabled her to focus all of her potential for an extremely productive life was never realized. That is a terribly painful thought for me and a loss to others.

Referring to the unrealized promise of children who die reminds me of one particularly bad moment during the last Christmas we had together. Laura Lue was trying to play a detached keyboard that someone had loaned her for the holidays, and she was doing it badly. Anger against illness that robs ability rose up in my throat; I thought I might scream out against a cruelty that diminishes. She would have played well had it not been for the leukemia. She did not even have a chance to go to her grave in full sail; she had to drift into port.

The loss of Laura Lue's worth to a world beyond myself was painfully heightened when I made my first pilgrimage to her grave. The marker had not been erected, and I was hardly able to locate her grave in the snow. I was stabbed by the thought that she had disappeared as well as died. In early spring I cut enough forsythia branches to blanket her entire grave with brilliant yellow blossoms. I seemed to have a need to establish the fact that she had lived. She had a right to her place in history that I longed to secure, even though she could not be an active participant in the future.

When people ask me how many children I have, I usually reply: "I have a son," if the inquiry is a casual one. If they persist and seem truly interested, I always say that I had two children, a son and a daughter, but that the daughter died at age ten. Then they usually apologize for being intrusive, and I say it is alright. I feel she must always be allowed the ten years she did have; I refuse to pretend that she did not exist just to make conversations less uncomfortable for other people. When I refer to the years when we were a family of four, I always indicate that, even if it confuses people who have only known me recently.

I must add, however, that I have never thought it right to import trouble to people who did not experience it. I almost never introduce the topic of her illness and death with people who do not already know about it. It is only with very select friends who shared those terrible times that I speak freely.

The world in general is impatient with those who grieve past a certain point. I remember a friend who was devastated by his wife's death and showed it for many months. Friends who were totally sympathetic at first became restive with his continued sadness and began to say: "____ should really try to shape up; he should be getting over this by now." I decided that they were not actually callous to his feelings, but that his slow healing meant they had to keep him on their list of concerns too long; there were other situations and people that legitimately demanded their attention. As long as he was visibly bereft, they could not "scratch him off their list," so to speak. I do not intend to be critical, just to state that people usually are able to grieve intensely with those who suffer a loss for awhile—but not for long. Only very special friends will be willing to stand by for the duration.

The hopeful thing I can say about the death of a child is that *one can survive.* I am sure that I said before Laura Lue was diagnosed with leukemia, "I could not endure the death of one of my children." I have heard many others say that. We all were speaking sincerely and truthfully according to our experience at the time. But I am on the other side of that horror now, and I know that survival is possible.

Even from the very first hours of my efforts to recover, I realized that Laura Lue loved life more than anyone I knew, and that to abandon life—productivity, growth, sharing, happiness—would be to dishonor her and despise the thing she loved and wanted. Not that retreat into a world of not loving anyone and, therefore, not being vulnerable to hurt was not a seductive thought. But after rolling that tempting apple around in my head for a time, I realized it was the coward's way out.

I recall that a friend spoke to me hesitantly about his daughter as if he had to apologize that she was alive and well while Laura Lue was dead. I sensed his dilemma and spoke directly to him about celebrating the life all around us that we still had. Once before that, while we were in one of our many residences in the hospital, another friend had stopped in the middle of telling me about his daughter's medical problem—as if it were not worthy because it was not life-threatening. I tried to free him to worry about her anyway. The living must seize the drama, joy, and pain of all the moments that are given to us.

Can I offer anything to those who mourn or seek to comfort those who mourn? The first thing to acknowledge is that I can only speak about what did and did not help me. There is as much variety in our modes of grief as in our appearance. Those persons who say, "I know just how you feel," are fantasizing. I can only humbly offer some suggestions to those who would be comforters and to those who grieve.

To Those Who Seek to Comfort

Twenty-five cents in the meter is worth ten "if there is anything I can do, just let me know." Laura Lue was treated in a university hospital in downtown Louisville, Kentucky, and I had to leave her room periodically to put money in the parking meter. Usually it was risky for me to go away even for a moment, because one of the courses in medical school teaches young doctors how to lurk around corners until the parent leaves the room so they can make their rounds at that instant and thereby avoid answering troublesome questions. (I am only kidding just a very little bit. It seemed to be on purpose because it happened so often.) But sometimes a friend would drop by to say he or she had seen my car outside and put a quarter in the meter. That was so much more concrete and valuable than vague promises for the future, and it demanded no effort on my part to search for them, perhaps unsuccessfully, later.

Yards need mowing, and household chores need doing; life goes on. Soon after Laura Lue had taken her last breath and the word of her death had begun to spread among our friends, I happened to look out the window of our house and see two young men, who were members of the Sunday School class I taught, out in the snow quietly shoveling a pathway to our house so we could come and go and others could make their way to us to offer comfort. They never even rang the doorbell to take credit for what they did.

Letters are often much more helpful than phone calls, particularly if the recipient has a large circle of support. After a long day at the hospital I sometimes came home to numerous phone calls, all from deeply concerned friends, but that were emotionally draining for me. After having lived the trauma all day, I was forced to relive it over and over again in the evening to bring the callers up to date. But I could read letters when *I* was ready—not whenever the phone happened to ring—and they required no immediate response on my part.

There are some blessings to collect even in the most terrible times.
Our family was the recipient of many such blessings. During the really
bad times in the progress of the illness, I knew we had crowds of people cheering for us. The doctors and nurses were giving us their best.
Countless people prayed for us, wished us well, and helped us in various ways. That graciousness was a healing salve on the wound of pain
and loss. And there was the cleaning woman at the hospital who
would ask, when she came in to mop, how the night went. If we could
answer that we made it through alright, her "Thank you Jesus!" was
like a blessing.

**A surprising amount of encouraging words and condolences are not
very helpful.** Sometimes words meant to heal were like knives tearing
into my flesh. I think of the person who said to me as I stood in front
of my dead child's casket, "You are young; you can have other children"—as if personalities are interchangeable instead of unique, and
one child is as good as another. And then there were those who heav-
ily implied that if we had only had enough faith or prayed correctly
that she would not have had to die. Those comments were all devas-
tating to hear. And yet I know that the people who said them had
good intentions.

All efforts to comfort and soothe were good-willed, and I tried to
take them as that. Printed cards let me know that our plight was of
concern to the sender, but of little other value. Even one sentence
composed by the sender is better than twenty printed cards. A handful
of extremely insightful letters was deeply beneficial.

The children from Laura Lue's class wrote letters that were absolutely beautiful and could serve as models for anyone. They were brief
and direct and did not pretend to more wisdom or involvement than
was actually present. One said, "I liked Laura Lue. I am sorry she
died." That was strangely comforting.

Keep your visits brief. A child in the hospital does not want the parent to spend a long time entertaining guests in the sickroom, so keep
visits as brief as possible or talk to the child.

Give meaningful and lasting gifts in honor or memory of the child.
It brought me joy to learn of gifts made in Laura Lue's name to

research, the Louisville Children's Hospital, and other good causes, including the planting of a tree in Israel by the Irving Rosenbaums. It was a way that her suffering was partially redeemed.

Include the child in his/her regular activities. Laura Lue's school, Emmet Field Elementary School, was wonderfully gracious in keeping a place for her during the long periods in which she could not attend class. I had to pick her up from school on September 23, 1969, for a test at the hospital, and she could never return except for the time we took cupcakes to her class in November to honor her birthday. She wore her new wig and was bright and lovely while we visited. When I tried to return Laura Lue's Suzuki violin to the principal, Miss McKee, she told me to keep it, that it belonged to Laura Lue as long as she might use it. I returned home gratefully clutching the violin as an emblem of hope.

Be open with children about their friend's illness, and help them to continue the friendship. I am unendingly grateful that the parents of Laura Lue's friends did not take the easy way out and manipulate their children to "forget" about Laura Lue, whom they must have strongly suspected was a terminal case. Instead they made the difficult explanations that allowed their children to keep in touch with us. On the very afternoon when Laura Lue was dying, Ann Potts, her friend on our street, and her mother walked down to see if Ann could play with Laura Lue for a little while. It is marvelous not to be abandoned.

To Those Who Mourn

Keep a record of your feelings. The single most helpful thing I did for myself was to write down my feelings after Laura Lue's death. I kept a daily journal until I did not need to keep it any longer. It was really in the form of a letter to Laura Lue. For one thing, I had an overwhelming desire to communicate with her. (I kept wishing her ghost would appear to me.) The other value in writing down the experiences of her illness and death and "talking" to her about them was that I could then release them. Before I began to write, I was constantly rehearsing episodes in the hospital and other traumatic experiences in minute detail, times when her pain might have been lessened if only I had battled the medical routine harder or—whatever, and on and on. I seemed destined to repeat those painful memories endlessly, but once I had composed the words on paper, my mind was composed also and more at peace about those memories.

Grief causes emotional, mental, and physical changes. I was relieved when someone with experience told me that I was not succumbing to a strange malady when I lost my sense of taste. I remember exactly where I was when I lost that sense and when it returned. I also read in a very helpful book that persons in grief often experience unusual mental and physical fatigue. It was of considerable reassurance to hear that I might not be falling apart, even though I had trouble concentrating or working for long periods of time.

Maintain physical exercise. Physical exercise was a real boon during the whole experience of illness and death. Louise Buchanan came many times to stay briefly with Laura Lue when she was really ill and I was on twenty-four-hour duty. In an hour and a half I could dash to the ice rink where almost no one knew me—and therefore I did not have to answer any depressing questions—get physically exhausted skating, and then dash back home. It was certainly one of the things that saved my sanity and health.

Allow yourself to experience normality. I learned to celebrate my enthusiasms as they slowly returned after Laura Lue's death. For a time I could not value or want any *thing*. My mother taught me by example when she did something very symbolic. She bought a chair that she had admired in an antique store, just to prove to herself that she could actually *want* something again and that our lives would go on.

Celebrate remembrances. From the beginning I have made Laura Lue's birthday the major time of remembrance. Penny and Rick Laughlin have been faithful and joyful in sending flowers to Crescent Hill Baptist Church in her memory to enhance the celebration of her presence in my life. I acknowledge the anniversary of her death and am deeply grateful to those like my son Rowan, who took the role of comforter from the beginning, and Carole Hovde and others who are very close, who are unfailing in remembering it with me. But I principally emphasize the day Laura Lue arrived instead of the day she left. It was a marvelous relief when Howard Hovde wrote to me on that first birthday without her presence, saying that November 11 would always belong to Laura Lue; it was her day. There is an enhancement for me in its being a worldwide holiday; everyone joins me in celebrating her on that day, even though they do not realize it.

Allow recovery in your own way and in your own timing. I was determined to recover in my own way and on my own timetable. One well-intentioned friend called very soon after Laura Lue's death, insisting that I start "getting out" right away. Others did not understand why it was a comfort to me to tend her grave or keep some of her clothes and treasures. One thing I am very sure of is that, though suggestions from thoughtful friends are helpful, each one of us needs to be free to choose our own method of healing and will recover best when we follow our own instincts.

Allow yourself to express emotions. I learned not to be thrown off-balance by sudden tears. When I least expected it, I would often be overwhelmed with sudden emotion and be crying before I knew it or why in particular I was crying. But those times have gradually subsided. In spite of all the pain, I can say unequivocally that I would relive every moment, if given the chance, just for the privilege of being with Laura Lue. It was a joy to have known her. I would not have missed her for anything—even the nightmare of her illness and death.

Faith, family, friends, and music offer great healing. Without faith it seems that I could not go on. My family is small but very loyal, and I am grateful to have many kind and caring friends.

When I was a young girl visiting an uncle, S. P. Williams, I watched him cope with the sudden unexpected death of a close friend. He sat for a long time listening to the New York Philharmonic Orchestra on the radio. His comment to me was, "Sometimes only music helps." I can say the same. Music must be the quality of abstraction, removed from language and reason that heals.

* * * * *

In reading the words I have written on these pages, I notice a heavy sprinkling of the first person singular. That style of writing certainly has its limits, but perhaps it fits the challenge of trying to give others the benefit of my experience. This essay after all is a distillation of my memory and the "sense" I tried to make of it all. I can only hope that there will be some point of identity and some suggestion of a method for coping that will be useful to those who read these words.

If I could only say one thing to those in grief, it would be: "Keep putting one foot in front of the other, even when you cannot see where you are going or tell that you are making progress in any direction." It is only by "keeping on" that we finally come into the sunlight again.

CHAPTER 3

❧ Needles and Thorns ❧

Harold N. West, Jr.

Leukemia is a disease of the blood. All humans have blood. Any human can potentially develop some form of leukemia. Leukemia is non-discriminating. Children are beautiful, and children are pitiful in equal doses. Shiny bald heads, both black and white, develop sudden attachments to various hats. Moms and dads cry colorless tears.

Cancer doesn't care about special days, holidays, or holy days. It doesn't care what you believe in, or who you believe in, or if you believe in anything at all. It doesn't care if you go to church on Sunday or play golf. It doesn't care if you are a king or a beggar. It doesn't care if you are an elected official or part of the elect of God. It doesn't care if you have a degree in philosophy and a diploma from Harvard or if you have the brain of a snail.

Beneath all epidermal and sociological layers are human hearts that beat as well as break. Our hearts were broken in February, 1981, when we heard the word leukemia used in the same breath with Philip, our three-year-old son. Broken hearts and shattered dreams. That, in part, describes our lives that day.

My wife, Elliott, and I shared many dreams concerning Philip, just as all loving parents do with their children. We dreamed about the kind of young man he might become. Would he be athletic? Would he be studious? Would he be a leader among his peers? We dreamed about what kind of talents he might possess and the college he might attend. We dreamed big dreams for him and for us! We dreamed about his career. Would he be a doctor, or a lawyer, or a preacher? It really didn't matter. We simply dreamed of his happiness and success, which would, of course, make us happy and feel successful.

I dreamed of the day he would publicly profess his faith in Jesus Christ. What a joy it would be to baptize my own son into the faith! Legitimate dreams. They may be prejudicial parental dreams colored with pride, but they are nonetheless good. And I somehow believe that if parents don't dream good dreams for their children, children have a difficult time dreaming good dreams for themselves.

That same week in February, our second child, Laura, was born. She was a beautiful baby. We were so happy to have a son and a daughter, and Philip was excited to have a sister. Life couldn't have been better, and the flow of our lives was positive, prosperous, and progressive.

The day after Laura was born, I was taking Philip to his grandmother's house so that I could go to the hospital to visit with Elliott and the baby. I noticed as we walked to the car that Philip was limping, and he didn't feel well. He seemed subdued and sluggish, not his usual energetic and lively self. I couldn't figure out why he was limping, and he couldn't tell me when or if he had hurt himself.

Later that week, I brought Elliott and Laura home. By that time, Philip had developed a fever. He stayed on the sofa in the den, where he was when we brought Laura home. He could only smile at her and hold her briefly in those initial moments at home. We thought Philip was experiencing another relapse of the mononucleosis he had first contracted during Thanksgiving. We had such a time getting him over that. We thought, "Here we go again!"

That week I took Philip to our family doctor. He was suspicious of Philip's joint pain and sent us to Philip's pediatrician. Philip was pale as a sheet, feverish, and could hardly walk. After examining several preliminary blood tests, the doctor sat down by me in the waiting area of the hospital, Philip's head on my shoulder, and said, "Hal, your son has one of three things: a continuing viral infection of some kind, rheumatoid arthritis, or leukemia. I want you to check him into the Medical University tonight or tomorrow morning. I'll make arrangements for you, and I want you to know that I have already been in prayer for Philip and for you and your family."

During the fifteen-mile ride home from the hospital that afternoon, I prayed and cried as it became clear to me that the worst fear of my life had a distinct possibility of coming true—losing a child to leukemia. As a child myself, I had seen a television show in which a young boy had leukemia and died. I had never forgotten that episode, nor had I forgotten that most people with leukemia die. The one thing I didn't want one of my children to ever get was leukemia.

Nevertheless, the very next day, a dreary February morning, a Jewish doctor, who would become like a brother to me and my wife, told me that his preliminary diagnosis, with further tests to be done, was that Philip indeed had some form of leukemia. Thus, with Laura less than a week old and Philip three weeks shy of his third birthday, the flow of our lives had been suddenly and drastically interrupted and altered. Nothing would ever be the same again, or even resembling the vision we had of our lives. Philip died nearly four and one-half years later.

The death and dying of children is one of the starkest proofs, if we needed it, that this world we live in is broken and sin-full and dreadfully unfair. The unfairness of our world is something we affluent Westerners would like not to have to face, but faced with it we have a difficult time dealing with it. We know the world isn't perfect. We can deal with the imperfections. We know that the world is full of sin, and we choose to deal with the sin or not. But we don't know how to deal with the unfairness.

I am one who has generally been on the advantaged side of this unfair world. As a fact of life, the majority of the people on this planet are on the other cruel and unjust side. I am convinced that most of us on the advantaged side have a generally distorted view of real life. We Americans in particular have come to expect that fairness is one of the inalienable rights of humans. For over 200 years, our people have been in a noble struggle over the fairness of society and its democratic laws. I think it is one of the things that has kept our nation alive, strong, and dynamic. But at some point, individuals in society must come to understand that fair laws and fair government and even fair attitudes of all our citizens cannot make life itself fair.

When things go our way, we think life is good and fair. It's not always easy, but we don't complain much about fairness. My father and mother are good Christian people. I grew up in a happy home. My parents were able to send all four of their children to college and graduate schools. Life wasn't unfair to them either. And then there is Philip, a product of prosperity, democracy, and opportunity. Was life fair to him? Did a good family prevent him from dying? Did democratic laws prevent him from dying? Did prosperity prevent him from dying?

Now, if you smoke three packs of cigarettes a day and get lung cancer, you can't complain on those grounds about the unfairness of life. If you drink a quart of whiskey a day and lose your job, your family, and your health and wind up destitute, don't complain on those grounds about the unfairness of life. If you sell your soul to cocaine and crack and lose control of your life to drugs, don't complain on those grounds about the unfairness of life. Suffice it to say that much of the misery and heartache of life is man's own doing through conscious choice. On the other hand, unfairness is known by the wives of many alcoholics, the parents and families of many drug users, and the families and loved ones of many persons whose life choices have brought them to ruin and death.

Since the first days of Philip's hospitalization, he was stuck more times than I can count, almost literally from head to toe. He had a Broviac line put into his chest and on several occasions was stuck with needles in the small veins on the top of his foot and many, many times in his back, arms, pelvis, and legs.

The life of a child with cancer is a life of needles, blood tests, chemotherapy, bone marrow tests, and lumbar punctures. One thorn after another producing pain, anxiety, fear, dread, resentment, tears, and blood. Philip knew the unfairness of life. He knew the unfairness of being hospitalized for days at a time. He knew the unfairness of being isolated from friends and people because of fear of infection. He knew the unfairness of feeling bad and feeling sick more days than not for four and one-half years. He knew the unfairness of having to guard his play because of low platelet counts and the fear of hemorrhaging. He knew the unfairness of struggling with school life and school work. He knew the unfairness of being bald many times and being chubby because of the effects of chemotherapy. He knew the unfairness of the regimen of pills and pain and the relentless necessity of needles.

I have a peculiar dislike for briers and thorns. While quail hunting in the Low Country of South Carolina, I have, on more occasions than I wish to remember, found myself in the middle of a brier thicket being literally pierced all over with thorns that can penetrate even the heaviest of protective clothing. Chasing quail into those forbidding thickets is a painful quest. I'm talking about brier thickets taller than the average man and so dense that you can't even get the old pointer to go in. That's why you're there to start with! I've learned that once you've committed yourself to one of those thorny thickets; there's no turning back, and there's only one way out: to plow straight ahead, stopping with nearly every step to loose your hands or legs or some other part of your anatomy from the angry grasp of thorns.

Perhaps only hunters understand this, but it's a parable of life. I would love to have hunted quail with a good bird dog on a clear crisp day in Paradise. Brier thickets and thorns would have been absent from God's creation and from the garden God so carefully planted.

Can you imagine the beauty and balance and bounty of Paradise? Can you picture the sunsets Adam might have seen? Can you fathom the fields of wild flowers Eve might have strolled through on spring mornings? Can you imagine the clarity and purity of the streams from which they drank? And when you consider all the abuse and destruction people have wrought in their time on earth, and that you can still find places on this planet that remain breathtaking and spectacular to behold, how magnificent and literally indescribable Paradise must have been!

It appears to me that Adam and Eve were not aware of the treasure of Eden. I suppose they had no way of really knowing the value of a "thornless" world until they lost it. And so it seems ironic that only in the act of sin did they come to appreciate the gift of Eden.

Nothing in all of the Bible explains the condition of humans and the presence of thorns in the world better than the third chapter of Genesis. It took the Lord two chapters to give an account of God's self as creator and companion of humans; and it took 1,187 additional chapters to describe human sin and God's attempts to redeem persons out of their brokenness, corruption, and destiny to destruction.

In part, the Lord said to his original rebels:

> Cursed is the ground because of you; in toil you shall eat of it all the days of your life; thorns and thistles it shall bring forth for you; and you shall eat the plants of the field. By the sweat of your face you shall eat bread until you return to the ground; for out of it you were taken; you are dust, and to dust you shall return. (Gen 3:17b-19)

There is little doubt in my mind that from then on Adam slovenly toiled on a tough and rough terrain just to survive. I can imagine that more than once, as he fought to keep control of his plot, he recoiled in pain and had to remove one of those thick thorns from his hand or from beneath a fingernail. The world had become a world of thorns.

The Bible is replete with a theology of thorns. God gave Adam and Eve the Garden of Eden, but they ended up with something far less. God gave the chosen people the land of Canaan, and although not Paradise, it was a land flowing with milk and honey, a good land. In the land dwelt the Canaanites, a pagan and idol-worshiping people. This posed a real threat to the spiritual welfare of the people through whom God would send a savior to the world. Therefore, God gave explicit instructions that the Canaanites should be driven from the land completely and that their statues, images, and altars were to be destroyed. But God added:

> If you do not drive out the inhabitants of the land from before you, then those whom you let remain shall be as barbs in your eyes and thorns in your sides; they shall trouble you in the land where you are settling. (Num 33:55)

Of course, that is exactly what happened. For much of its history, life in Canaan was a life of thorns and thistles, when all the while God had something so much better in mind. Rebellion again took its toll.

The thorn is an appropriate symbol of the price of sin. Consider these verses from the book of Proverbs: "Like a thornbrush brandished by the hand of a drunkard is a proverb in the mouth of a fool" (26:9). "The way of the lazy is overgrown with thorns, but the path of the upright is a level highway" (15:19). "Thorns and snares are in the way of the perverse; the cautious will keep far from them" (22:5).

Thorns, the enemies of God, are no match for the fire of God's judgment: "I have no wrath. If it gives me thorns and briers, I will march to battle against it. I will burn it up" (Isa 27:4). And the writer of Hebrews equates the unbeliever to one who grows thorns and briers: "But if it produces thorns and thistles, it is worthless and on the verge of being cursed; its end is to be burned over" (Heb 6:8).

Thorns afflict often by choice. We may choose to walk into the brier thicket and thus invite pain and sorrow into our lives through rebellion and the pursuit of power, pleasure, and prominence. But all too commonly thorns afflict us by chance while we devotedly follow the good and pursue the beautiful, reaching for a rose but instead, reeling in the pain of a thorn in the flesh. The presence of thorns on roses is an illustration of our beautiful but dangerous world. Philip was not the recipient of the judgment of God because of his choices. He was the recipient of a deadly thorn because he was born into a world of sin, hatred, disease, war, and death.

The apostle Paul had "a thorn in the flesh" that, though not deadly, must have constantly reminded him of the unfairness of life. He asked God to heal him three times, but the word came back: "My grace is sufficient for you, for power is made perfect in weakness" (2 Cor 12:9). I am confounded to know why God would not oblige this relatively simple request by a man who taught others to walk by faith and not by sight, a man who upon examining scripture never put a limit on faith. Paul was a man of similar passions with us, but I am convinced that it was not a lack of faith that prevented the thorn's removal. Consider what this tenacious, old warrior had been through.

By his own account, he had often been imprisoned and near death. He had received severe whippings at least five times. Three times he was beaten by rods. He was stoned once and left for dead, and he endured three shipwrecks. As he said, "In toil and hardship, through many a sleepless night, hungry and thirsty, often without food, cold and naked" (2 Cor 11:27). A thorn in the flesh? This man was in some kind of physical pain that, though he asked the Lord to heal him, he had to live with. Paul came to understand that many thorns would not be removed, even from the flesh of people of faith.

Philip had been in remission for about a year when I received an anonymous letter in the mail at the church. In essence the letter asserted that when I had enough faith, God would heal Philip.

When I go to prayer, I have had a heavy burden for your son Philip. If you will only believe your son will be healed. But because of your unbelief he must suffer. Please read Mark 9:14-29.

When he [Jesus] came down off the mountain, he didn't find an atmosphere to work in. He found confusion. He found people arguing. He found people questioning. He found people at complete odds with one another. But here in the midst of all the confusion was a man that had a demon-possessed son that had a need. What did he do? He separated himself from the bunch of unbelievers.

And if you want God enough, you will come to him individually, personally, and say, "Jesus I've got a need." He said "My little boy has got a devil and I brought him to your disciples, and they couldn't cure him." Now listen to this! Then Jesus asked him a question. "How long ago is it since this came unto him?" And he said, "Of a child" (Mark 9:21). He said, "But if thou canst do anything, have compassion on us, and help us." Jesus told him (in so many words), "You've got it all backwards. It's not if I can do anything." Jesus said to him, "If thou canst believe, all things are possible to him that believeth" (Mark 9:23).

Then the father cried out with tears, "Lord I believe, help thou mine unbelief." And Jesus rebuked the devil, and he departed out of him, and the child was cured from that very same hour" (Matt 17:18). That father had been caused to doubt so much that he even doubted whether Jesus could do it or not.

It's the truth! It's a true statement today all over America and the world. There is so little of the Word being preached. Good people really don't realize it, because God cannot confirm the words of Henry Wadsworth Longfellow. He cannot work a miracle through the writings of Helen Keller. He cannot open a blinded eye through the gallant sayings of Shakespeare. Instead of saying, "As a man named Shakespeare once said," we need to start saying, "As a man named Jesus once said!" And start believing it, start confessing it, and start receiving it.

I will keep travailing for your son in prayer until you believe that Jesus Christ will heal your son.

Needless to say, the letter upset me. The writer, who did not have the courage to sign his/her name or speak to me personally, seemed to place the burden of Philip's illness and suffering squarely on my shoulders and blame it on my "unbelief." The fact is, I had believed from the beginning that God would heal Philip. I prayed for it unequivocally everyday. We prayed together. We prayed as a family. We prayed as a church and a community. People of many faiths were praying earnestly. We received encouragement from people all across the country. People and churches we knew nothing about were praying for Philip's healing.

After reading the letter through several times, I began to recognize certain things about it that led me to believe that a certain young lady, a new Christian whom I had baptized, had written the letter. She had lately been drifting from our fellowship into another group and had suddenly become more "spiritual" than the rest of us. I filed the letter away, but never said a word to the suspected author. I believed then, as I do today, that the faith of a mustard seed can remove mountains, but sometimes not thorns.

Central to a theology of thorns is the cruel crown of thorns that Pilate's soldiers crammed on Jesus' head. As a precursor to the crucifixion, one can only imagine the pain of many thorns jammed into the scalp that precipitated the flow of Jesus' precious, atoning blood. To me, the crown of thorns is at the very heart of all I feel and believe about the unfairness of this world and the death of children. In all of Jerusalem, in all of Judea, in all of the world, there was no more innocent a person to wear that crown than Jesus of Nazareth. He wore that crown for all of us. He wore that crown for the most animalistic of men, and he wore that crown for the sweetest of children.

As I think about Calvary, my mind goes back to the summer of 1984, a year before Philip died. We had a funeral at our house. Our faithful little dog of twelve years died. We decided that a proper burial was in order. Philip and I carefully constructed a plywood coffin of calculated proportions and reverently placed our beloved little Cockapoo inside and solemnly nailed the top shut. We then picked out an appropriate burial plot among some camellia bushes and dug a grave.

As were our plans, we then summoned Elliott and three-year-old Laura outside to attend the funeral service that consisted of a few moments of reflection about our departed pet and words of testimony, not to mention several questions from Laura. Then we had a brief prayer, thanking God for giving our family such a special friend and family member. I will never forget as I began to cover up this tiny coffin that Philip took off into the house without saying a word. I finished pushing down the damp, loose soil, and Elliott and I were trying to console a crying daughter and answer that same old question of, "But why did she have to die?"

I remember we were sitting on the ground near the grave when Philip darted out of the house, ran by the three of us, and timidly threw an object in our direction. When I picked it up, I couldn't believe it. I nearly burst into tears myself. Philip had secretly and compassionately constructed a cross of two sticks he had found and bound them together with some scrap pieces of yarn. We called him back and praised him for caring enough to take the time to lovingly make a cross to put on top of the little dog's grave.

As I have stated, I don't know how much Philip understood about death, and I'm not sure how much he understood about the cross, but I believe he had an idea that the cross was more than simply a sign of death and a grave marker. I want to believe that in making that cross he was comforted and strengthened, and that for him some of the pain of losing an object of love was lessened when he saw the cross standing above the grave where lay the body of his friend.

That episode was a blessing in a way. It was a traumatic experience for Laura, but in less than a year she would be faced with the death of her older brother. Watching as we covered the coffin with dirt and said our final good-byes, experiencing the aura and impact of death was a preparatory prelude to things to come.

Calvary was God's answer to a world of thorns, a world of sin, a world that loves death and hates life, a world that maims and destroys the innocent and worships the malevolent, a world that crucifies the Son of God and deifies the devil. Thank God, there is triumph over the thorns! God promised that the Word was sent to do a job, and it would do it. The Word would not come back empty-handed. God first promised this through the prophet Isaiah in the context of restoring the children of Israel to Judea. God made them a promise of mercy, reconciliation, and pardon. In verses 6 and 7 of chapter 55, Isaiah declared these powerful words concerning the promise:

> Seek the Lord while he may be found, call upon him while he is near; let the wicked forsake their way, and the unrighteous their thoughts; let them return to the Lord, that he may have mercy on them, and to our God, for he will abundantly pardon.

And so in the context of these overtures to the Jews in exile, God promised a new beginning. The Word would accomplish it:

> So shall my word be that goes out from my mouth; it shall not return to me empty, but it shall accomplish that which I purpose, and succeed in the thing for which I sent it. For you shall go out in joy, and be led back in peace; the mountains and the hills before you shall burst into song, and all the trees of the field shall clap their hands. Instead of the thorn shall come up the cypress; instead of the brier shall come up the myrtle; and it shall be to the Lord for a memorial, for an everlasting sign that shall not be cut off. (vv. 11-13)

God's Word has succeeded. There was a triumph over the thorns. There was reconciliation and restoration. The people did return to the Lord and to the land, but the triumph was not a lasting one. Another Word must come. A final Word must come to bring ultimate mercy, reconciliation, pardon, and triumph over the thorns. That Word came in the form of the Son of God. God sent His Son to do a job, and he did it. Jesus knew it and so declared from the cross before he died: "It is finished!" He did what he came to do: to break the power of sin in the world, to atone for the sins of humans, and to triumph over the thorns of the world and the last enemy (death).

The prophet Ezekiel also spoke of a new day, looking through and beyond the restoration of Israel to a day in which God will make all things new:

> The house of Israel shall no longer find a pricking brier or a piercing thorn among all their neighbors who have treated them with contempt; and they shall know that I am the Lord God. (28:24)

John recorded God's promise this way:

> He will wipe every tear from their eyes. Death will be no more; mourning and crying and pain will be no more, for the first things have passed away. And the one who was seated said, "See, I am making all things new." (Rev 21:4-5a)

The Word became flesh and dwelt among us. He was born in the brier patch of earth. He felt the sting of thorns all his life. He grimaced when they pressed the crown of thorns upon his head. He reeled when they impaled him on the cross. But he triumphed over the thorns. He arose from the grave. He returned to the Father having completed the job he was sent to perform. God's Word, the Logos, did not return void. The innocent victims of thorns are now exalted victors with Christ. That is how we think of Philip, and that thought sustains us through the pain that lingers still.

CHAPTER 4

❧ Gentle Whispers ❧

Richard S. Hipps

In 1992 our family was completing ten years as missionaries to Brazil. It had been a wonderful decade. Our three children, Justin, Lacey, and Alexandra ("Alex") were especially looking forward to furlough. It had been five years since we had been in the United States. In fact, little Alex would be meeting most of her family for the very first time.

A church near Atlanta, Georgia, was generous enough to allow us the use of its missionary residence. My wife, Patricia, continued her studies of the German language at the Goethe Institute in Atlanta while I commuted back and forth to Harvard Divinity School. Having been named a visiting scholar in Christian ethics, I was especially interested in researching the near-death experiences of children.

The subject of near-death experiences is certainly controversial, and I felt that we needed more than philosophical, psychiatric, and psychological studies. We needed pastoral, theological, and ethical inquiries as well. One writer in particular has intrigued me. Diane M. Komp, a pediatric oncologist and professor at Yale University School of Medicine, was either an agnostic or an atheist until one of her little patients changed her life forever.

In her book, *A Window to Heaven*, Komp tells the story of little Anna who was dying of leukemia at the age of seven. Before she died, the little girl sat up in her bed and declared: "The angels—they are so beautiful! Mommy, can you see them? Do you hear their singing?" Then she died. Commenting on Anna's death, Dr. Komp made this observation:

> Her parents reacted as if they had been given the most precious gift in the world. The hospital chaplain in attendance was more comfortable with the psychological than with the spiritual, and he beat a hasty retreat to leave the existential doctor alone with the grieving family. Together we contemplated a spiritual mystery that transcended our understanding and experience. For

weeks to follow, the thought that stuck in my head was: Have I found a reliable witness?[1]

Why did that hospital chaplain miss a wonderful opportunity to discuss with Anna's parents their child's dying words, her angelic visitation, her precious gift? Could it be that he was uncertain about what "spiritual ministry" really is or how it contributes significantly to a person's well being?

In this post-modern era, some ministers have become so secularized that they function more comfortably in a psychotherapeutic role than in a spiritual one. Yet, when we ministers fail to speak in God's name or offer some expression of the sacred transcendent, those seeking our help may feel slighted, misled, or even disillusioned.[2]

For whatever reason, the pastoral-theological-ethical aspect of ministry seems to have diminished in favor of a clinical-psychological approach. Many have given way to the temptation to become therapists more than ministers. A lot is being said about transactional analysis, developmental psychology, and a variety of other quasi-pastoral interests; but little theology is being discussed. Taking their directions from non-theistic guides, many ministers, like Esau, "have sold their theological birthright for a bowl of pottage called psychotherapy."[3]

Can This Really Be Happening?

February had been unusually bleak. We had hoped for a good snowstorm, because little Alex wanted to make a snowman. Having lived all of her life in Brazil, she had never seen snow. What we got instead was rain, severe thunderstorms, and tornadoes.

I will never forget Sunday evening, February 21, 1993. A tornado touched down five miles from our little missionary residence. We were all huddled in a closet next to the chimney while the tornado warning signal was blaring at the nearby fire station. We had left Alex in her bed just a few feet from the closet, ready to grab her if necessary because she had been so sick that day. A terrible flu had made its way through our family, but had been especially hard on her. Our physician had to change her medication because she gagged every time we tried to give it to her.

The tornadoes passed, but Alex's flu did not. For the next two days she grew weaker, unable to keep anything on her stomach. The doctor, fearing that perhaps she was dehydrating, instructed us to take her to the emergency room. After checking in, we were told by one of the nurses that several children had recently been admitted because of this flu. We were assured that after adequate hydration she would begin to feel better. Petrified of needles, Alex offered very little resistance. She was just too weak to fight. At about three o'clock in the afternoon we were told that we could take her home.

As she tried to sit up, the nurse noticed that her blood pressure dropped dramatically. Concerned, she called the physician back into our little room. He knew then that we were dealing with something other than the flu. There would have to be more tests. The first thing would be a spinal tap to check for meningitis. We could not be with her during that test.

Standing outside in the hallway, we heard her screams and fought back the temptation to open the door and walk in. Having hardly spoken above a whisper for several days, she was now mustering what little strength she had to vocalize the pain and fear she felt. When we were finally allowed back into her room, she was totally exhausted. Holding her little bear (Beary), she cried softly. So did we.

"I Want to Go Home"

Alex was moved to the intensive care unit around 9:45 P.M., because her blood pressure continued to be very erratic. Although several physicians were now studying her case, none could give us concrete answers. They kept telling us, "We just have to wait, monitor her closely, and see what happens."

Throughout the night Alex drifted in and out of sleep, restless with all of the sophisticated equipment taped to or stuck in her little body. The catheter was especially uncomfortable. Patricia and I stood by her bed, caressing her, telling her everything would be alright. When she drifted off to sleep again, I pulled two chairs up close to her bed. We had been on our feet for hours.

A few minutes later Alex did something very unusual. She opened her eyes very wide and stared at us in such a strange way. It was a look we'll never forget. Her eyes began to move around the room slowly and deliberately. She was so pensive. After a minute or two she looked at her mother and said, "Mommy, I'm scared." We both stood up and placed our hands on her little body. Patricia said, "Darling, you don't have to be afraid. Mommy and Daddy are right here with you."

Once again Alex very contemplatively surveyed the room. Turning those beautiful blue eyes in our direction, focusing on our faces, she said with warm emotion in her voice, "Jesus is here too." Not understanding the significance of her statement, we very casually replied, "Yes, sweetie, Jesus is always with us."

At around 5:00 A.M., Alex looked at me and said, "Daddy, I want to go home." I continued to rub her leg and said, "It won't be long; don't worry." Only a few minutes passed, when all of a sudden she jerked backwards violently, and her little heart stopped beating. Patricia and I were rushed out of the ICU, and a medical team began working with her. They did all they could to get her heart to start beating again, but to no avail. When the chaplain entered the conference room where we were waiting, we knew that she was gone.

About half an hour later, the attending physician entered our room and confirmed what we already knew. He added, "We honestly don't know what happened. Would you give us permission to do an autopsy?" Of course, we agreed. It was later determined that a disease called myocarditis, an inflammation of the heart muscle, had taken our little girl's life.

One Day at a Time

Lying is easy; telling the truth is hard. Let me tell you the truth about losing a child. Nothing in our experience prepared us for such a staggering blow. It has been the most agonizing ordeal we have ever faced. It is a loss that simply can't be fathomed. Surviving the death of a child is a day-to-day task. Some days I think I'll make it; other days, I'm not so sure. I have reached levels of depression I never knew existed. For the first few months, grace and grit were my only props.

As a husband, father, brother, pastor, and friend, I have people who love me and need me. I have made peace with the fact that I have no choice but to endure Alex's death and go on. God has been good to Patricia and me in never allowing both of us to be down at the same time. It seems that when I've been at my worst, she has been at her best. In her bad days I have added strength. Also, helping Justin and Lacey work through their grief has contributed to our healing.

We have walked with the Lord for a long time. Serving God in ministry has been the consuming passion of our lives. Our hope has always been in Jesus, not in our well-made plans. He never promised to give us answers; he only promised to be with us. There have been times when we've felt lonely, but we've never felt alone.

In his book, *One Small Sparrow*, Jeff Leeland chronicles his ten-month-old son's struggle against a fatal bone marrow disease. The reader is given a graphic account of the medical torture this little boy had to endure as well as some very good theology.

> When our boy was journeying through the valley of the shadow of death during his transplant . . . we no longer felt God's hand . . . But it was then we felt his heartbeat . . . It was then we realized most deeply that He is a personal God who weeps, who is acquainted with every sorrow, who has ached with our every pain.[4]

I've spent too much of my life trying to make sense of everything that happens. It's taken me years to learn that some things don't make sense. Some questions don't have answers. In the words of Gilda Radner, the comedienne who died in 1989 with cancer, "Some poems don't rhyme, and some stories don't have a clear beginning, middle, and end.[5]" I now plan to spend the rest of my days in a "holy resignation," believing that the Lord does indeed love me with an everlasting love and has my life in divine hands. Trusting God has become more important than understanding God.

We introduced our children early to C. S. Lewis' *The Chronicles of Narnia*. In the fourth book, *The Silver Chair*, a little girl named Jill finds herself lost in a scary forest. She cries so much that she develops a tremendous thirst. Looking for water she finds a stream, but a lion is lying beside it. The Lion, knowing she is thirsty, invites her to come and drink.

> "May I—could I—would you mind going away while I do?" said Jill.

The Lion answered this only by a look and a very low growl. And as Jill gazed at its motionless bulk, she realized that she might as well have asked the whole mountain to move aside for her convenience.

The delicious rippling noise of the stream was driving her nearly frantic.

"Will you promise not to—do anything to me, if I do come?" said Jill.

"I make no promise," said the Lion. Jill was so thirsty now that, without noticing it, she had come a step nearer.

"Do you eat girls?" she said.

"I have swallowed up girls and boys, women and men, kings and emperors, cities and realms," said the Lion. It didn't say this as if it were boasting, nor as if it were sorry, nor as if it were angry. It just said it.

"I daren't come and drink," said Jill.

"Then you will die of thirst," said the Lion.

"Oh dear!" said Jill, coming another step nearer. "I suppose I must go and look for another stream then."

"There is no other stream," said the Lion.[6]

Whatever Happened to Heaven

My godly grandmother told me a story I'll never forget. When she was about ten years-old, she had prepared some food for her father who was working in a rock quarry. Her mother had died four years earlier, and my grandmother not only assisted in the preparation of meals, but helped to rear her younger brother.

To get to the quarry she had to cross a long bridge over a river. Granny, as we called her, was terrified of the bridge. On that particular day she was so overcome with fear that she sat down at the bridge and began to cry. Unexpectedly a voice said, "Honey, if you are afraid to cross the bridge, I'll walk with you." Standing by her was a man holding the reins of a horse. He looked quite normal, but in Granny's words, "His eyes were so bright and his voice so comforting."

No longer afraid, she walked across the bridge with the kind stranger and his horse. Their conversation was light, discussing specifically the beautiful blue sky. As they approached the end of the bridge,

Granny turned to thank the man for his company. And before her eyes, both man and horse vanished!

In the modern church, stories such as these are seldom heard. There seems to be an aversion to the supernatural. We have diluted our vision of heaven and lost interest in God's invisible kingdom. We resist any notion of transcendence and are emphatic about finding our fulfillment in this life and no other. We have become masters at keeping our distance from the intangible. Nevertheless, our belligerent attitude often exposes an inner turmoil.

I admire the noted writer and Bible translator, J. B. Phillips. It took courage to write some of the things he wrote. He put his impeccable reputation on the line by admitting that he was visited by the deceased C. S. Lewis not once, but twice. The first visit was while Phillips was watching television. Looking up, Phillips saw Lewis sitting in a chair just a few feet away. His ruddy complexion and glowing health made him look "large as life and twice as natural." Lewis spoke briefly about some difficult circumstances Phillips was facing.[7]

One week later while reading in bed, Phillips was visited by Lewis again. This time he seemed even more robust and radiant. He repeated the words he had left with Phillips before. What were those words? Twice Lewis told Phillips, "It's not so hard as you think."[8] As Christians we live by faith and not by sight, but God has blessed us with some special "insights" that are difficult to explain. I call them "gentle whispers."

After Alex's death we decided to remain in the United States and not return to Brazil. We had to buy a house because the church I now serve did not have a parsonage. The very first house we were scheduled to look at seemed perfect. It was in a good neighborhood. There was a lake and a playground nearby. The house had four bedrooms. The fourth bedroom would have been for Alex, but would now be used for our many guests.

We knew that this was meant to be our house when we entered it the very first time. Going upstairs we began to examine the bedrooms. One of the bedrooms stood out. It was painted the ugliest color of aqua you can imagine. This just happened to be Alex's favorite color. We never could understand why she loved aqua so much. Now we do.

God was reminding us that she *is* with us because God is with us, and "He is the God not of of the dead but of the living" (Matt 22:32).

Another "gentle whisper" was that for several weeks before Alex died she kept reminding us of things we had forgotten, things we had enjoyed together in Brazil. She was steadfast in asking, "Do you remember?" It was as though she was refreshing our memories to give us strength for the journey.

God is my witness, but as I write these words I am listening to a tape I made from a radio program in Brazil. I love Brazilian music and wanted a good supply for furlough. I just happen to be listening to the one I made in July 1991. At the end of the tape, the music stops and a little voice says, "Come to supper, Daddy, we're having chicken." It is Alex's voice. Her mother had sent her to get me, and "for some reason" I had recorded our conversation. You can call it coincidence. I know better. Why did this occur at the very moment that I'm discussing "gentle whispers"?

I can assure you that I'm not in denial. Nor am I stuck in one of the many stages of grief. I grieve as deeply as anyone who has buried a child. I simply long for more than this world has to offer. The "joy that is set before me," the hope of heaven, helps me to endure. It keeps me going.

Hear me well. Just because I yearn for heaven does not mean that I devalue this present life. There is still a lot of living to do on this earth. Our family is not the same since Alex's death, but we're still a family. Patricia and I look forward to seeing Justin and Lacey grow up and lead happy, fulfilling lives. We want to spoil our grandchildren while continuing our ministry for many years to come. Our desire for heaven actually enhances our lives here on earth. Peter Kreeft expressed it this way:

> Throughout history it has been precisely those who believed most strongly in the next world who did the most to improve this one. That's what you would expect. If you believe the road you're on goes nowhere, you don't take it too seriously. If you believe it goes to somewhere important, you keep it up.[9]

Perhaps what we feel is best described by words taken from a Carmelite monastery in Waterford, Ireland.

I have only slipped away into the next room.
Whatever we were to each other, that we are still.
             Call me by my old familiar name,
speak to me in the easy way which you always used.
             Laugh as we always laughed together.
             Play, smile, think of me, pray for me.
Let my name be the household word it always was.
             Let it be spoken without effort.
             Life means all that it ever meant.
             It was the same as it ever was;
             there is absolutely unbroken continuity.
Why should I be out of your mind because I am out of your sight?
             I am but waiting for you, for an interval,
             somewhere very near just around the corner.
                          All is well.
             Nothing is past, nothing is lost.
One brief moment and all will be as it was before—
             only better, infinitely happier and forever,
             we will all be one together with God.

Notes

[1]Diane M. Komp, *A Window to Heaven: When Children See Life in Death* (Grand Rapids MI: Zondervan, 1992) 28-29.

[2]Benedict M. Ashley and Kevin D. O'Rourke, *Health Care Ethics: A Theological Analysis* (St. Louis: Catholic Health Association of the United States, 1982) 399.

[3]Robert H. Albers, "Current Developments in Pastoral Care," *Word and World* 6 (Spring 1986) 208.

[4]Jeff Leeland, *One Small Sparrow* (Sisters OR: Multnomah Books, 1995) 217.

[5]Gilda Radner, *It's Always Something* (New York: Avon Books, 1990) 268.

[6]C. S. Lewis, *The Silver Chair* (New York: Macmillan, 1953) 16-17.

[7]J. B. Phillips, *The Ring of Truth* (New York: Macmillan, 1967) 118-19.

[8]Ibid.

[9]Peter Kreeft, *Fundamentals of the Faith* (San Francisco: Ignatius Press, 1988) 69.

CHAPTER 5

❧Sunshine and Shadows❧

Julian S. Orrell

A rthur J. Gossip was one of Scotland's great preachers. Perhaps he is best remembered for a sermon he preached entitled "But When Life Tumbles in, What Then?" This was the first sermon Dr. Gossip preached after his wife's sudden and untimely death. Probably the most moving line in this highly-personal sermon is found in these words: "You people in the sunshine may believe the faith, but we in the shadow must believe it. We have nothing else."[1]

One cannot help but be reminded of Peter's words as he confessed both his own inadequacy and his strong faith in the Christ: "Lord, to whom can we go? You have the words of eternal life. We have come to believe and know that you are the Holy One of God" (John 6:68-69).

Life is not fair. The cross was not fair. The fairest flower that ever blossomed in this universe was put to death by cruel and self-seeking people. Crucifixion was the most horrible form of death known to humankind. It was forbidden for Roman citizens to die by crucifixion. And, yet, the cross turned out to be God's saving redemptive deed for all who would believe in and surrender to the Christ.

Moreover, when sinful persons had done their foul act, an almighty and loving God turned it all around on that first Easter morning. Disciples who were totally discouraged on that black Friday long ago—the hub had been removed from the wheel—those disciples who had been lurking in hidden-away places, were nerved with new courage. And they went up and down the length and breadth of the land proclaiming a risen Savior who is alive forevermore, a Savior who made ten appearances to individuals or groups of individuals during the forty days between his resurrection and ascension.

What does all of this have to do with our lives? The answer is "everything!" We go through life—even to the age of seventy as we did—enjoying countless blessings, and even assuming erroneously that we somehow are immune to heart-wrenching suffering. But that is not the way our days play out. No one is immune to suffering, not even our Lord. Since we are not immune to suffering, the pertinent question is: "How shall we handle suffering when it suddenly descends on us from the rear?"

On the night of November 20, 1994, our tranquil world was shattered; time stood still at 9:30 P.M. We received the terrible news—the heartbreaking news—that our younger daughter, our son-in-law, and our grandson had been involved in a head-on crash with a drunken driver. The woman driving the truck had crossed the center line, giving our son-in-law no opportunity to avoid the collision.

The driver was killed upon impact, as was our twelve-year-old grandson. Our daughter was severely injured, but has recovered sufficiently to return to teaching her class of active fifth-graders. My son-in-law was suffering from multiple and life-threatening injuries, and was evacuated by helicopter to Norfolk General Hospital. There, despite the efforts of an excellent trauma team, he expired on December 22. We had buried our grandson, our daughter's only child, on Thanksgiving Eve, and we buried our son-in-law on Christmas Eve! Our daughter's family was wiped out!

In the midst of our anger, we kept asking, "Why?" Since I have now lost an aunt, two fellow-pastors in the prime of their lives and usefulness, a precious and talented grandson, and a CPA son-in-law—all due to drinking drivers—I, of course, ask the question: "Why"? I'm afraid that I have a lot of questions—more questions than answers.

Are our legislators afraid to enact and enforce the tough laws needed to get drunk drivers off the highways? Are some of our legislators afraid that tougher laws might catch them? What about so-called "social drinking"? What about so-called "moderate drinking"? Again and again in my forty-seven years as a pastor, I have attempted to counsel alcoholics who began as "moderate drinkers" or "social drinkers." Why have we made the consumption of alcoholic beverages so fashionable and socially acceptable that we fail to deal realistically with the terrible carnage on our highways? We are simply losing too many innocent and valuable people, and we are losing them needlessly. These and many other questions linger. They haunt me and my wife of forty-seven years. ˙

We will never get an answer to all of our "why's" We have to move beyond anger and "why's," as did Job. Once stark tragedy has struck, and we have cried our buckets of tears, what then? Even though we know in our hearts that God's people are safe, as the book of Revelation tells us, how do we deal with the pain of physical separation? Our daughter's home is not very large and is very lonely.

Helmut Thielicke, the first Protestant to serve as rector of the University of Hamburg in Germany, reminds us in his book, *Our Heavenly Father*, that no one of us has to go through the dark forest of suffering alone. There is indeed one who has already come to our sides in the person of Jesus Christ. According to Thielicke, we have no right to make God the author of all evil and suffering:

> That is an utterly and completely unbiblical idea. On the contrary, what we have again and again is that the powers of sin and death and suffering are hostile powers, enemies of God. God did *not* will that they should exist.[2]

Many years ago Stewart Newman reminded us that God must have a great deal of difficulty being everything that we make God out to be.

The God of our Lord Jesus Christ did not cause that drunken driver to cross the center line and kill my grandson and son-in-law. This tragedy was emphatically the result of her decision to become intoxicated, and then get behind the wheel of a powerful Isuzu truck. She exercised free moral choice in a needless and totally irresponsible manner. Therefore, since there is no valid basis on which to blame God for this tragedy, how can God help us to cope with our grief and facilitate the process of healing? How can God help our daughter and our son-in-law's parents as we all go through these deep waters?

I am convinced, more now than ever before, that the living God revealed in Jesus Christ is with us in good times and bad times. Thielicke is on target when he writes as the Father speaks:

> Your sorrows are His sorrows; otherwise would I (the Christ) be standing here among you? He has sent me into the midst of your sorrows.[3]

And then the Son speaks:

> Every wound I lay my hand upon has ached a thousand times in me; every demon I cast out has leered at me; I died the death

that I myself defeated; I let my own body be torn and buried in the earth. Who among you suffers and I do not suffer with you? Who among you dies and I do not die with you? I am your comrade and brother in every pain, whatever your lot may be . . . God suffers pain for you and with you.[4]

For me, this means that no experience in all of life, even those experiences that are hardest and most difficult, has to be faced apart from a definite sense of the Savior's strong and abiding presence with us.

In his book, *A Spiritual Autobiography*, William Barclay tells the tragic story of his twenty-one-year-old daughter and her fiance, who were both drowned in a yachting accident. As Barclay states it,

God did not stop the accident at sea, but he did still the storm in my own heart, so that my wife and I came through that terrible time still on our own two feet.[5]

A critic asked him, "Where was God when your daughter and her fiance perished?" Barclay responded without hesitation: "the same place He was when His own Son died."[6] It is within this context, in the full knowledge that our grandson and son-in-law are at peace with Jesus Christ, that my family and I are attempting to deal with our grief. We find other sources of strength as well.

Sources of Spiritual Strength

The Holy Scriptures and Prayer. We are finding passages such John 14:1-21; 1 Corinthians 15:12-58; Psalm 103; Psalm 90; and Psalm 23 —all of which I have used many times in conducting funerals—to be more meaningful now than ever before. And we are probably re-reading them more now than ever before with a devotional mind-set. As we have our morning devotional time, my wife and I find God's living word speaking to our heart needs through the written Word. This entire experience has been a "reality check" for us. We have been driven back to the basics of our faith.

We also believe in the power of prayer. Fully aware that it does not always turn out this way, I will cite what I believe to be a classic example of answered prayer. On the day before our son-in-law died, my car broke down on Interstate-64 between Richmond and Norfolk, Virginia, as I was traveling to the hospital. I waited a good while in the cold, traffic rushing by, all the time praying and hoping for help.

Finally, a lady, who had initially passed me earlier, turned around on the highway and came back to help. I immediately showed her my clergy identification. She allowed me to make several calls on her cellular phone. Eventually I was able to start my car. She followed me all the way to my dealership where I left the car to be checked. Since the lady lived in Norfolk, she volunteered to drive me to Norfolk General Hospital where my son-in-law was dying. I later learned that on that very day a number of our dear friends in both Norfolk and Richmond had been praying specifically for me.

Fellowship with and Faithful Support of Friends. My wife has kept a record of the phone calls and cards we have received. The number of cards now exceeds 650! Simply to be remembered and supported by that many people has been extremely meaningful to us. Literally hundreds of people have prayed and continue to pray for us. I even learned a few days ago, as I lay flat on my back in the dental chair, that our dentist is praying for us! Every church we have served has been found faithful in loving prayer support. Dr. Raymond Spence and the entire staff of the Second Baptist Church in Richmond have been towers of strength to us.

A longtime Presbyterian minister-friend, whose children grew up just one block from ours, upon hearing of our grandson, Matthew's, death, warmed and lifted our hearts with the following tribute to him and our daughter, Frances, who goes by the name of "Dee Dee":

Budded on Earth Is to Bloom in Heaven

Your letter and clippings crushed our hearts today. We never knew Matthew, but because he was yours and Dee Dee's, we loved him from afar, interested in his health, life, and achievements. Now he's got his earthly journey done, just when we thought it was beginning. I'm so thankful God measures not in days and hours, but in love and spirit. Love and spirit transcend time so handily.

We are the left broken ones, and in the hurting, we exchange crosses and joys according to our lot and need. For Frances (Dee Dee) we feel a bond of love—this latest news has burnt like a branding iron her cause upon us. We will never think of her again without a pause to reflect upon this scar of loss upon her.

And the thought then goes to God's heaven where we will have time for everyone and everything—a privilege not enjoyed on earth. There we will really enjoy knowing Matthew and be as young and beautiful as he is in the Kingdom of our Lord Jesus Christ.

Earth's a mess. Thank you, God, for heaven, where life and happy relationships are not broken, love's bonds continue, but in heaven they won't be so frail. Love requires two, and you know your love is even in this world sustained by Matthew's from beyond.

R. D. Goshorn

Physical Exercise. My wife, Eleanor, and I have found that physical exercise helps to relieve some of the stress of the past two months. Even though as I write this we are in the dead of our Virginia winter, it helps to get outside and do some physical labor such as raking leaves, cleaning off the garden, cleaning the gutters, or walking (which is especially enjoyed by Eleanor). I love my garden, love to see things grow, and feel a nearness to the living God as I work in the soil. As soon as the weather warms, working in my garden will be wonderful therapy for body and soul.

Travel. We meet new friends and explore new horizons through our travels. My wife and I have been blessed in being able to do considerable travel, which we hope to continue. We look back now to a trip last spring, as we retraced the second missionary journey of the apostle Paul in Greece and Turkey. We relived his days in Athens, Thessalonica, Philippi, Corinth, Rhodes, Mykonos, and Ephesus. That trip further enhanced our appreciation of Paul and his faith in the Risen Christ. The Lord willing, we hope in another month to enjoy an Elderhostel in Florida, and possibly some additional partnership missions, either here at home or overseas.

Consolation and Conclusion

Even in the midst of our grief, my wife and I are consoled by the fact that our daughter, despite some serious injuries, is recovering from the crash and has been able to resume her teaching responsibilities. Had she been in the front seat of their car, it's highly unlikely that she would have survived. Also, our son-in-law's injuries were so serious that, had he survived, it is doubtful he would have been able to live a normal life. Even in the midst of tragedy we have cause for gratitude.

At the time when we were confronted by the double loss in our family circle, my wife was undergoing radiation treatment following two cancer surgeries. It has helped to remember God's humanity—and our humanity as well. I have a colleague in ministry who is fond of reminding us that we are human beings—before and after we become Christians.

Paul Tournier, the Swiss psychiatrist and physician, wrote these words in his book, *A Doctor's Casebook in the Light of the Bible*:

> It (the Bible) does indeed bring us the triumphal shout of faith, like that of St. Paul: "For me to live is Christ, and to die is gain" (Phil 1:21). But even the most lively faith does not spare man the anxiety of death . . . Fear of death is not lack of faith . . . To keep one's faith is not to be superhuman, to imagine that one is not subject to fear; it means rather admitting one's natural rebelliousness and confessing it, and receiving, thereafter, super-natural strength to overcome it.[7]

Among the many assurances of faithful support we have received, none has been more helpful than a card we recently received from a retired missionary friend:

> Give eternal rest to them, O Lord,
> whose souls have taken flight,
> And lead them to a better world
> where there is peace and light.
> Grant them eternal freedom
> from trouble, pain, and care,
> And fulfill for them Thy prophecy—
> there shall be no night there.
>
> Helen Steiner Rice

Notes

[1]Clyde T. Fant and William M. Pinson, Jr., ed. *Twenty Centuries of Great Preaching*, 13 vols. (Waco TX: Word Books 1976)8: 235.

[2]Helmut Thielicke, *Our Heavenly Father* (New York: Harper & Brothers, 1960) 25.

[3]Ibid.

[4]Ibid., 23.

[5]William Barclay, *A Spiritual Autobiography* (Grand Rapids MI: Eerdmans, 1975) 45.

[6]Ibid., 23.

[7]Paul Tournier, *A Doctor's Casebook in the Light of the Bible* (New York, Evanston, and London: Harper & Row, 1960) 163.

CHAPTER 6

❧ The Gift of Bryan ❧

Caralie Nelson Brown

A healthy, happy Bryan celebrated his third birthday on May 29, 1956. After eating his cake, he and his seven-year-old sister, Nancye, went with me in our old Plymouth, "The Bluebird," to a local amusement park. As they mounted the carousel, Nancye said, "I'm going to pretend I am Dale Evans." "I, Royde," chimed in Bryan, as he sat on his "horwie giddup." Then he "rode off" on "Trigger." As they went 'round and 'round, up and down, I waved each time they passed by and rejoiced in God's gift of such precious children.

The summer was filled with many activities for Nancye and Bryan: attending Vacation Bible School, playing in our backyard, and visiting my mother in South Boston, Virginia. We were also making plans for a visit to the Brown grandparents in Baker, Louisiana, in August, when my husband, Ray, who was pastor of a church in Richmond, would have his vacation.

Suddenly our world seemed to stop, and all plans were put on hold. Bryan was not well. After experiencing mild discomfort for several days, he began to suffer a great deal of pain on Saturday, July 21. It was necessary to call our doctor to come to our home. He was able to determine that Bryan had a mass of unknown origin in the abdominal region. We experienced agony as we lived through the rest of Saturday and Sunday. After a visit to the doctor's office on Monday, it was determined that Bryan would have to be hospitalized so that tests could be made to find the cause and nature of the mass.

After the necessary tests, a team of physicians decided that an operation was necessary, and it was performed on July 27. Still dressed in his green fatigues, the surgeon came into the room where we were waiting and said to Ray and me these chilling words: "The tumor was highly malignant. Bryan has about a year to live even if given X-ray treatments. The chances of his complete recovery are poor to fair." In the midst of the gathering storm clouds, there came a faint ray of sunshine with these words, "Some cases of neuroblastoma have been remarkable because the tumor has just disappeared."

Should we tell people that Bryan had only a year to live? We decided not to do so. We did not want to have Nancye living under such a cloud of despair. Maybe Bryan would be one of those who recovered completely. We agreed not to live a tragedy nor to burden others anymore than necessary. For Bryan's sake we felt it was imperative for us to live as normally as possible. We shared some of the news about Bryan's illness with relatives and friends outside of Richmond and with friends and members of our congregation in the city. The word spread rapidly in a community of caring. Flowers, cards, and toys came in abundance from those who wanted to show their sorrow and concern.

We received two kinds of mail: funny, cheerful cards addressed to Bryan, and comforting notes and cards sent to Ray and to me. What a source of strength it was to be assured that our relatives and friends were praying for us to be strong and for Bryan to recover completely! Communications came from childhood friends, college classmates, and ministerial associates. They came from people we did not know and from those to whom we were very close. I was overwhelmed by the goodness of people, by their thoughtfulness of our physical as well as our spiritual needs. Many to whom Ray and I had ministered were now ministering to us.

I sought help from the Bible as I looked for evidences of healing in the Scriptures. They were there as I had remembered: a high fever assuaged, leprosy cleansed, and a paralytic's legs restored. Faith and healing seemed so closely associated in the biblical accounts. Bryan was too young to understand his illness or to have faith that he would be cured. In Luke 7:1-10, I read of the healing of the centurion's servant. Here was a clear case of the faith of one person that helped in the healing of another. "Can I have faith for Bryan?" I wondered. "Dear Lord, please help me to have such faith for our son," I prayed. The words of another suppliant came to my mind and were formed on my lips, "Lord, I believe; help Thou my unbelief" (Mark 9:24).

The months following the initial operation were filled with despair as the tumor returned, but with hope as X-ray treatments reduced its size. Yet, there were wonderful experiences of joy as the Brown grandparents and aunts, Jean and Helen, came to see us during Thanksgiving season. Bryan was well enough to enjoy their visit and seemed at that time to be improving, prompting Helen to say to me, "I believe Bryan is going to get well."

In December our days were filled with preparations for Christmas. The children helped make paperweights with their pictures for several of our relatives. They participated in celebrations of the birthday of the baby Jesus. Of course, like all children, they anticipated their gifts from Santa most of all: a dollhouse for Nancye and an electric train for Bryan.

After the children were asleep on Christmas Eve, Ray and I assembled the train and set up the figure-8 track. The little engine looked so real as puffs of smoke came from the stack where we had dropped pellets. Putting Nancye's dollhouse together required more mechanical ability, and we labored on and on into the night. Finally "Santa" had come and all was ready for Christmas morning.

It seemed that the children were up before we had even dozed. "How it work?" Bryan asked when he saw his train. Ray showed him how to push the lever, and he was soon "driving" his train like a real engineer. Nancye was taking "a tour" through her dollhouse, rearranging the furniture. The children tore into their other packages under the tree, and the living room looked as if a strong breeze had turned over the contents of several trash cans.

Laughter, squeals of delight, bits of conversation, and the click of the train floated into the kitchen as I prepared breakfast. Suddenly, my mind was pierced with the barbed thought, "Was this our last Christmas together with Bryan?" "Oh! Father," I prayed, "don't let such a thought cloud our present joy." My prayer was answered.

After an examination by the doctor in January, it was evident that the tumor was increasing in size again. X-ray treatments began again on January 30. Despite our prayers and those of countless friends, it was apparent that Bryan would not be healed of the malignancy.

Through Bryan's illness, I had grown in my devotional life to believe that the power of God could heal incurable diseases. Now I must have the faith to believe that God is all good and all powerful, even though Bryan would not be healed. I was being sustained by the comfort of Almighty God, the tender love of Ray, and the concern of friends and family.

On February 25, we were given the prognosis that medical science could do nothing more for Bryan except to keep him comfortable. Despite his illness, Bryan continued to play most of the time. Occasionally he would say, "I feel better now." Only then did we realize he had been in pain. Even when he was confined to the bed, he liked to play. He wore his Davy Crockett outfit or his Roy Rogers clothes. I read to him, sang with him, and played with him, as did Ray and Nancye.

On March 28, Bryan had to return to the hospital where he underwent another operation on March 30. A colostomy was performed for the elimination of his body's solid waste. Because Bryan was so ill, we decided that Nancye should not visit him in the hospital. Perhaps this was not a good decision, but we thought it was best at that time. Nevertheless, Nancye "visited" him in her own way. She made little bookmarks and sold them to our neighbors to get money to send to Bryan.

While I was straightening Bryan's hospital room and rearranging some of his possessions on the bed on April 8, he said, "You can have all my toys." I thought my heart would burst. I fought back the tears. Did he know he was dying? I do not know. It was the only thing he ever said to indicate he would not play with his toys again.

Though Bryan expressed no thought of going to heaven, there had always been a certain quality of spirituality about him. Once he told me, "God is the best man in the world." When he asked a blessing at mealtime, he often kept his eyes open during his prayer, surveying the food on the table, and mentioning in his thanksgiving each dish he saw.

On April 10, Bryan's kidneys ceased any function, and the doctor said he would live only twenty-four hours and would possibly go into convulsions before the end. The days passed. Bryan did not die as predicted, and he had no convulsions. It was a miracle.

Since there was a special nurse to care for Bryan, I went home each evening so I would be refreshed to be with him in the daytime. So it was that I went home on the night of April 16. At 5:17 A.M. on April 17, we were awakened by a phone call from the hospital. Bryan's condition was worse.

We dashed to the hospital and were met at the door of Bryan's room by the nurse with these words, "He just stopped breathing." He looked as if he were asleep. I leaned over to kiss his warm little cheek. "Oh, darling, I didn't want you to die without me," I thought. "I failed you. I should have stayed last night." I stopped these thoughts. I had done all I could do. Ray was praying The Lord's Prayer, and the nurse was joining with him. I could not speak, though I could pray. When Bryan was alive, I never wanted to leave his room. Now that he was gone, I did not want to stay.

As we drove home from the hospital, I said, "Ray, you will have to tell Nancye. I won't be able to talk." When she awoke, Ray held her in his arms in the living room as I sat beside them on the sofa. He beautifully explained that Bryan's body was diseased and God had given him a new body. God had taken Bryan to his heavenly home where he could play and never suffer anymore. It sounded so beautiful. Then Nancye simply asked, "But is he dead?" Ray answered, "Yes." She jumped off his lap and ran into a corner of the dining room, sobbing. I went to her and held her in my arms. I could not really comfort her. We could just cry together. So profound was her grief that she scarcely ate anything for several days.

Bryan's funeral was held at Tabernacle Baptist Church on Good Friday, April 19, with Ray preaching the sermon. I do not know how he did this, but he did. It was his gift to Bryan he told me, and I knew it was also his testimony of faith to his congregation. Near the close of his message, Ray said,

> We cannot go around suffering, but we can go through it. The way winds to a hill called Calvary and through an empty tomb and ends at the right hand of God. All glory of Easter is ours today on this Good Friday! In loving gratitude and in holy faith we now give up our son, not to death, but to a living Christ. There will be a bright tomorrow—our Lord Jesus will bring it.

"With the dogwood trees a fairyland and the azaleas bright with bloom, we walked across the rich green grass of spring and laid . . . in the ground"[1] all the earthly remains of Bryan. As we left Westhampton Memorial Park in Richmond, we knew that our stewardship of his little life was continuing, not ending.

How could we live with the memory of Bryan's life and his untimely death? There were many options: to live despairingly, bitterly, fearfully, flippantly, or resignedly. But Christ taught us his way. We must live with our loss redemptively. Through God's power we must enter more fully into the sufferings of others and point them to the Healer.

Of course, in our humanity and weakness, Ray and I often cried, "Why?" The months after Bryan's death did not give us the answer, nor have the almost-forty years since provided any real explanation for me. These words that Ray wrote a year after Bryan died continue to comfort me, however: "God gives no answer to suffering; He gives Himself."[2] "Thanks be to God for his indescribable gift" (2 Cor 9:15).

Notes

[1] Raymond Bryan Brown, *The Fire of Truth*, Richard Spencer, ed. (Nashville: Broadman Press, 1982) 21-22.

[2] Ibid., 120.

CHAPTER 7

❧Our Journey through Grief❧

Walt and Elizabeth Barnes

February has always seemed like a cold, dreary month to me—too far past the holiday excitement for it to be a fresh memory and too far from spring to really be hopeful. This particular February in 1989 goes far beyond dreary. I am numb, robot-like, beyond depression. I sleep as much as I can, barely able to be counted as one of the living. I do only the absolutely necessary: eating, bathing, communicating on a minimal level with family and friends, walking an old sick dog, trying to keep the Grim Reaper from claiming another victim close to me.

Days seem to blur into oneness. No one day has any distinguishing features from another—except for Saturdays. On Saturdays, we dress warmly, pack up our little space heaters, and head to what must surely be purgatory. In this instance, purgatory has an address: a building that once housed a car dealership in Wake Forest, North Carolina. The building is deserted at this point, but not for long. It will soon be transformed into a Western Auto, so our purgatory, in its physical sense, is going to be short-lived.

The gray bleakness of the maintenance portion of the building fits right in with my color scheme for purgatory. The lack of any regulated temperature in the car bays only adds to the shiver I feel as I enter. Our reason for being here is utterly bizarre: all our earthly belongings have been stored here. They are wet, in most cases ruined, and totally valueless, except to us.

We come here to sift through the remnants, compile unending inventory lists for the insurance company, and make irrational decisions about what to cling to. As I sit and write at the makeshift table, Walt, Chip, and Liz bring me items to log on the list; and then we decide the fate of each one, agonizingly. We have no rationale behind any of our decisions. At this point, nothing makes sense.

Back in November, in the days leading up to Thanksgiving, almost everything made sense. We were the stereotypical American family: a son in his sophomore year in college, a sixteen-year-old daughter harassing us about a driver's license, and a nine-year-old third-grade daughter running for student council secretary at school. But that was before Thanksgiving.

Our lack of uniqueness changed forever on the Sunday night after Thanksgiving. Chip flew back to college, and we drove home that Sunday from a family holiday visit in Tennessee. The two girls, Walt, and I drove until late that evening. Interstate traffic was predictably terrible at the end of the holiday weekend. We took a break an hour from home and stopped at Hardee's. Afterward, the girls climbed into the back seat and instantly fell asleep as we began the last leg of our journey together.

As we drove into our subdivision, I remember our conversation focused on the fact that in only one week we would attend our church's Hanging of the Greens Christmas ceremony. I asked the girls if they knew what they were supposed to do. Janet self-assuredly noted that she had her words and music memorized and was totally ready.

We never heard her sing those words. . . . At 1:10 A.M., I was roused from a deep sleep by an unfamiliar noise. As it grew louder and more ominous, I shook Walt and urgently asked what it was. He very groggily answered that he didn't know. Before I could do or say anything else, our Armageddon arrived. Something gripped our house and shook it like a half-empty box of cereal. The background music was the smashing of glass, a deafening roar, and my question to Walt, "What about the girls? What about the girls?" All the while my eyes were tightly shut, clinging to Walt as though we were on a roller coaster at a theme park. Then it stopped as suddenly as it started. I wanted off this ride!

I opened my eyes to the most unbelievable sight: thick, black electrical wires menacingly hanging down close to us, the bookcase leaning over our bed, its contents violently spewed over the room, windows blown out, rain falling in, and most noticeably, everything now graveyard quiet.

Walt began to get up, and I desperately pleaded with him not to. We made it through the event, whatever it was, and I was frantic at the thought of his being electrocuted as I watched. He sternly told me he must get up. About that time, we heard Liz beginning to call Janet's name. We joined in.

We got up only to find our door blocked by a huge pile of bricks —where *did* they come from? By this time the three of us were climbing over debris, moving whatever we could, still calling, waiting for Janet to answer.

As we entered Janet's room, we noticed that the view was panoramic—no roof or walls. We were looking into the night sky. I looked at where her bed had been, and it was no longer visible under the rubble. An hour before, I had checked on her as I went to bed. She was peacefully asleep in her white French Provincial canopy bed. A lovely child. But entering her room now, I knew she could not have survived the crushing weight of the fallen chimney.

The feeling that accompanied my realization was one of strange acceptance, as though a giant hand gripped my shoulder and a voice said, "She's OK." After all, that is a mother's main concern: is my child OK? At the time I could not string together the logic of her being alright and yet not seeing her there, but I had the overriding sensation that she was fine. From that moment until now, I have never doubted it.

To our amazement, we learned during that marathon night that a tornado had unyieldingly forced its way into our lives. Without our consent, we were stripped of our definition of family, of physical security, and most of all, of Janet.

Elizabeth's Perspective

Looking back now, I find it has not been so much the events of that one night in November with which I have wrestled. Rather, it has been the everlasting, ever-droning implications of the event that have driven me to unbelievable depths of despair. In the beginning, the agony lay in my child being so irreverently snatched from me, with no chance for appeal, no forum for argument, and worst of all, no time to say good-bye. The only consolation I ever found was that I would not have wanted to know what lay ahead. God must surely know the limits of our endurance.

We quickly found that death is not always a lone raider but can be the first of a gang of marauders. Very soon after Janet's death, we were told that 85 percent of parents who lose a child in death end up divorcing. I remember screaming silently in protest, "Do we have to *lose everything?* Wasn't she *enough?*" Having spent countless amounts of time in the quicksand of sorrow, we have been able to see how this could happen.

Grief is such a very, very personal torment. It cannot be shared in total by or with another person. In the case of a married couple, they may both be dealing with the loss of the same child, but the vestiges of personal loss that a father feels for a child differ from those of a mother bereft of her child. The other surprising element of a couple's grief is that it totally absorbs each person involved in it, leaving them very little to give to the other, despite what they might want to do. Grief is indeed the loneliest game in town.

Walt and I went through the throes of grief at the same time. In that sense, we were very much together, but in actuality, we were very much alone. We could talk about the loss, about Janet, about what we were feeling, but we experienced a sense of real helplessness because we were totally unable to help each other. We realized that if we had had any other issues between us (unresolved conflicts, brooding resentments, and so on), we might not have made it through the grief intact as a couple.

We have characterized a scenario in which a couple sweeps issues under a rug throughout their relationship, rather than dealing with them. When the rug is suddenly stripped away (by the death of a child, for example), the issues are laid bare, demanding resolution. The loss of a child on top of other significant marital tensions often requires more personal resources than two people can muster. The issues can be eliminated by dissolving the marriage, but nothing can be done with the grief.

Another very strong reaction I experienced was the veiled, unconscious expectation of another personal disaster. My not-so-subtle goal was to ward off the next tragedy by finding it before it found me. Looking back, I detect an implied sense of guilt because I had not foreseen disaster the first time. I wanted to control every possible situation to avoid being blindsided again.

Being totally preoccupied with scouting for our next encounter with destiny resulted in a significant lack of concentration and not surprisingly, resultant memory problems. I then became convinced

that I had Alzheimer's disease because of my symptoms, which neatly
fit into my expectations.

I was often asked if I felt angry toward God about Janet's death.
Surprisingly, I felt that God was my beneficiary as far as Janet was
concerned. I was convinced that Janet was in God's loving care, a care
much more adequate than mine could ever be. It made no sense to me
to be angry at God if I was entrusting Janet to God's care. I also never
held God accountable for what happened. A loving father does not
hurt his children.

Less than a month after Janet's death, we were in K-Mart shop-
ping. It was unusually hard to stay in the store with the flood of
memories that overwhelmed us. Walt left the store, but I wasn't ready
yet. I proceeded to walk up and down the toy aisles where Jan had
spent her time. I had to be sure she wasn't there. It was a desperate
thing to do, as though I believed some mistake had been made and I
would find her there. The more I looked, the more despondent I
became at not finding her.

In a flash, a thought struck me so profoundly that it molded
my perspective immediately and permanently. I went to the car
chuckling. Walt, in amazement, asked what was so amusing. My
response was, "Our daughter is with the Creator of the universe,
and I want to bring her back to *K-Mart?*" I understood then that
my grief was for *my loss,* not for Janet in her new situation. This
experience was graphic because it also demonstrated my slowness in
accepting the finality of her absence. My gradual acceptance of the
inevitable took months, maybe years, not days or weeks.

We tried in small ways to be proactive during the healing process.
We agreed that we would never avoid difficult situations. We became
determined to deal with our grief head-on rather than avoiding it. As
a rule, this approach worked quite well. We never ran from people,
places, or memories, but rather walked right through the midst of
them. It was not easy, but we learned we could do it on a day-by-day
basis. This built confidence in our ability to keep going.

I found a surprising outlet in composing several piano pieces during the first couple of years. Although they oozed with grief, hurt,
hopelessness, intense sadness, and total despair, they nevertheless gave

me an outlet I could go back to over and over. Only one of them was light and joyful, and it was written to depict Janet's persona.

One of the most serious phases of our grief came upon us quietly and overwhelmed us before we were aware of its presence. This phase was best characterized with one overriding question: "What's the point?" For a somewhat prolonged period of time (perhaps as much as a year or more), our response to every event, every thought, every plan, every impulse was that one simple question. We could find no reality with any purpose, and we decided to simply trudge through each day, hoping to stumble into meaning somewhere along the way. During this period of dismal hopelessness, I developed a strong cancer wish as my legitimate ticket out of this reality.

The caring of two particular friends made a difference to us during that time frame. As a couple, they embraced us with persistent love and caring, insisting that we join in activities or simply spend a quiet evening with them. We never wanted to go, but they would not take no for an answer. Our load was never as heavy on the way home as it was when we arrived at their door.

As the years began to pass, I noticed another unusual response on my part. I never let Janet stop growing and developing in my mind's eye. With each birthday that passed, she became older to me. I would wistfully think of what she would be like, how she would look, and what she would be doing. I have never been able to leave her at nine years-old. Walt, however, has never been able to picture her any older.

Walt's Perspective

My first overall response was to accept the event and loss in reverence and silence. There was simply nothing to say, not even "Why us?" Why *not us?* I knew that as I held Janet for the last time, she on one side of death and me on the other, God was taking care of us both.

During the weeks and months after her death, my mental and emotional breakers constantly shut down as a built-in protection to keep reality from driving me insane. As time passed, however, these breakers shut down less frequently, permitting depression to gain its foothold. I began to think about why reality exists as it does. If God is all-powerful and all-loving, why does God allow such pain to exist? More and more I raised questions. Though I very firmly believe that God neither kills children nor ordains such events as God's will, this nevertheless took place in a reality that God created. Why?

I never once worried about Janet. My developing struggle was about my grief, not about Janet's situation. I became more stern and direct with my questioning. Finally, I was screaming at God with my fists clenched, demanding an accounting for such a flawed universe. How could God permit this to happen under God's watchcare?

In grief's throes, I screamed out in agony and despair! I found I didn't have to be gentle with God. God could handle my tough questions and my anger. The questions I asked were not answered directly, but I found that God loved me enough to hold me while I hurt and grieved. God understood this grief; He lost a child, too.

It seems, all too often, that many sincere, devout people feel they somehow must protect God from their grief and anger. By holding in their emotions, they are not demonstrating faithfulness but rather, showing a lack of it. Peace is only possible after struggling through emotional encounters with God. If we have to tip-toe around to protect God from our puny wrath, our perception of God is too small.

My life became filled with an ongoing echo of emptiness caused by Janet's death. It became the only medium in which my life could be lived. It was apparent that my entire existence had been inexorably changed. I never wanted to go to sleep because upon waking each morning, I was immediately and brutally crushed by the shock wave of my loss—*she was* dead. I felt I had been dragged into court and given a life sentence with no possibility of parole.

Grief was an unbearably heavy backpack forced upon me, with skin grafted over the straps. Removal was impossible. On countless occasions, I would pray for strength to survive the next five or ten minutes without losing my sanity.

In times like these, communication becomes so very important. Because grief is such an individual process, the strength required to maintain this personal struggle often destroys one's ability to keep sight of loved ones who are also suffering. This process of self-isolation can happen so gradually and subtlety that it may be missed altogether. Therefore, it is vital to call out in the darkness to those we love, to remain in earshot, if you will, to maintain contact, however difficult it may seem.

Our Present Perspective

Looking back over the last seven years, people and events have come into much clearer focus. The response of hundreds of people who sought to provide us with physical and emotional warmth is overwhelming to say the least—everything from a condominium for temporary living quarters to a magnificent picture of Janet that occupies a central point in our home.

Friends and strangers who reached out to us with tear-stained faces, expressing their own anger, bewilderment, and sorrow, always amazed us. We never expected others to hurt with us as they did, but their grief provided us with strong assurance that we were not alone. The warmth, compassion, and presence of our church family have been especially significant in our healing process. We have experienced ministry at its best from our congregation.

Having received so much from so many, we find our response centers on wanting to give back something to others. There have been times when we prematurely tried to give, and our well simply was not deep enough. Over time, however, we have found we have been able to do more, and the satisfaction from doing so is immense. This process for us will be an ongoing one.

We still do not have answers for all that happened, but answers are not central to us now. Knowing that God is ultimately in control of everything provides comfort in the midst of the questions. We know that God was never beyond our reach, and that God's love and care for us never wavered, especially in the storm. The mystery of life has been magnified, but so too has the peace that has come from struggle and acceptance.

We have never stopped including Janet in our family. Each family gathering is a time to re-tell Janet stories. We laugh and find great joy in the tales of things that were, and then we gently pack the memories away until the next time.

A special treat for us is hearing stories from other people. Friends, acquaintances, and, on occasion, even strangers have shared with us some encounter they had with Janet. These newfound treasures are added to the wealth that Janet bequeathed to all of us. Her best friend, Lara, is especially dear to us. She has cherished Janet's memory even as she has grown up, moved away, and started a new life. We are amazed that a girl so young would possess such a mature understanding of loyalty and friendship.

We realize that we did not give up everything. We still have two wonderful children who provide us with so much joy and love. Our families have been loving and caring, special friends have warmly embraced us along the way, and our relationship has strengthened to provide us with a base from which everything else makes sense. Priorities have changed. Material things are inconsequential; family relationships have greatly escalated in importance.

We find that our encounters with depression are less frequent, but they still hurt as badly as before. The difference is that we now know these are single points in time, not representative of the whole of our lives. We still find it easy to drift toward despondency and inertia at times, but we have learned to better control this tendency together, each keeping watch over the other.

We have discovered that the bottom line is this: there is no short-cut through this harrowing process. The only way around the issue is straight through the center of it. Life looks more normal to us now, although never the same as before. Time has ever-so-gradually loos-ened the grip of grief. Much of the intense despair and anguish has slowly faded . . . like the sound of a train whistle moving away in the distance. In the stillness, though, the echo of our loss is ever present. The weight in the backpack is less, but the straps are still grafted securely. Parts of this reality can never change.

We find that we have changed so much, both as individuals and as a couple. Our sadness comes from realizing, however, that our growth is in response to this tragedy. But why couldn't we have grown some other way?

CHAPTER 8

❧ "Yes" to God's Call ❧

Charlene Andrews Ray

Many years ago I heard my mother-in-law say, "I don't want to live to see another of my children die." She had lost three babies and a six-year-old child. She had five grown children remaining. She was in a nursing home at the time. The oldest son did indeed die before she did, but by that time her mind had deteriorated to the point that she did not realize it, for which we were thankful. Years later I came to understand her plea.

On the morning that our daughter, Susan, died, my husband and I sat outside the hospital room with her doctor and nurses. We all watched as the hospital emergency team tried in vain to revive her. We told her doctor, "We have both said to ourselves that we must outlive Susan. We couldn't bear to think of her having to manage without us." We had cared for her almost every day and night for forty-five years. Her brother and sister-in-law had assured us they could take care of her in the event of our death or disability. But we couldn't imagine how they would be able to do it with their other responsibilities.

You see, Susan was a respiratory polio quadriplegic. She slept in an "iron lung" (tank respirator) every night and used a positive-pressure ventilator during the day. She could use neither her arms nor legs, except minimally, and her diaphragm was completely paralyzed. Her only unassisted breathing was accomplished by "frogging," a glossopharyngeal breathing term, descriptive of swallowing air like a frog.

My husband and I felt in our hearts that Susan must go first. Yet, when Susan said to me during the last night of her traumatic hospital stay, " I think I'm dying," I went to bed and prayed, "Oh Lord, not now! Not now!"

During the early morning hours the next day, the emergency crew rushed into the room, pulled her "iron lung" out into the light of the hallway, and started resuscitation efforts. Those persons watching her heart monitor said it was erratic: perfect on one, weak on the next. The pneumonia was under control, her heart rate was more stabilized . . . but the Lord said, "It is now."

Susan was stricken in February, 1952, during the last spell of the polio epidemic. The Salk vaccine was being tested that summer. After four or five weeks in our local hospital in Lubbock, Texas, her doctor secured an entrance for her into Southwestern Poliomyelitis Respiratory Center in Houston, Texas. We traveled by military plane with Susan in a portable tank respirator designed by a doctor at Brooke Field in San Antonio. He used it to transport polio-stricken servicemen home from overseas.

When we arrived at the Center, a team of nurses and aides met us. They were obviously knowledgeable about what to do. Since we had all worked with Susan in Lubbock mostly by instinct, we were relieved to turn our daughter over to those who seemed so capable.

My husband returned home to Lubbock to his pastoral duties. My mother and father arrived the next day with our baby son, Lanny. We rented an apartment and settled in for an indefinite stay. I could visit Susan only on Wednesday and Sunday afternoons. But as summer came on, the polio epidemic grew worse. I volunteered to help in the children's ward because the nurses and aides seemed so overworked. I was allowed to help out eight to ten hours a day.

Susan seemed to be making little, if any, progress in being able to breathe outside the "iron lung." I was so discouraged that one night I prayed, "Lord, if you will let Susan live, we will try to rear her in such a way that she will be useful in your service. And if this can be, give us a sign." When I went to the hospital the next morning, one of the nurses said, "Come look what Susan can do!" I peered in through the window of her tank. Susan was barely moving one leg! It was the sign!

When I called my husband to report the good news, he said he had had a similar experience. We knew then that the Lord had something for Susan to do! Soon she was able to tolerate a chest shell respirator and be out of the tank for perhaps an hour in the morning and an hour in the afternoon. But when the doctor tried her on the rocking bed, a very minimal breathing aid, she could not tolerate it. They had to rush her back into her tank.

Finally the Center became so crowded that the doctor told me, "We have to send someone home. And since you've been working here so much, we think you folks can manage at home, even though Susan is still confined to the tank for at least twenty hours a day." "How long do you think she can live?" I asked. Dr. Pheiffer replied, "Perhaps three to six months."

Soon after Susan's fifth birthday in July we were taken home in a military air transport plane. With Susan inside, her big Emerson tank was strapped down out in the middle of the otherwise empty plane. A moving van took us to our little house in Lubbock, and Susan was moved into our small living room. We were home.

Right away my husband began his "equipment building." He was determined that, along with her chest shell respirator, Susan must be able to "rock." After an old hospital bed was turned into a "rocking bed," Susan was given a "try." It was a couple of months of daily "trying" before she could do more than a few minutes, but finally she could do thirty minutes twice a day.

In 1956 my husband was asked to take a job in San Antonio as director of missions for the Baptist association. We moved there in the spring of Susan's third year in school. And since San Antonio did not have a schoolteacher for homebound children like Lubbock had, I became her teacher. At the school where our son, Lanny, would go in the fall, I was given all the text books we needed—along with much encouragement.

I was told that San Antonio schools required Spanish in elementary school. We were almost three books behind already! Since I had studied Spanish for two years in high school, I took the first, second, and third grade books. Susan and I studied all three books before school was out. The Lord was preparing her for a special work.

By that time, my husband had already built many pieces of small equipment to fit Susan. A small tank respirator had replaced the big Emerson. We made her first check-up trip back to Houston in it. She also had a small rocking chair to replace the rocking bed. She went to church in it on Sunday mornings and "rocked" for an hour in the aisle. A multiple-use chair could have the "bed" part moved from the small wheel base for inside use to a bicycle wheel base for outside use. A small "travel" tank allowed us to make trips outside Texas. We had become truly mobile and pioneers in travel for respiratory "polios."

Mike Mojica and his family became our very close friends in San Antonio. They even bought a house across the street from ours. Their

two sons and Lanny played together. And their daughter, Becky, along
with Cheryl from down the street, came to visit and play with Susan.

One summer the Mojicas and our family decided to attend a conference at Glorieta Baptist Assembly in New Mexico. I had observed
that Susan seemed to have an aptitude for writing, and we decided the
Writers Conference at Glorieta would be a good experience for her.

We all enjoyed the Writer's Conference, and Susan got to attend
some of the youth meetings as well. During one of these meetings
Susan made a commitment of her life to work with Spanish-speaking
people. Neither she, nor we, knew how she would accomplish it. But
if God called her, God could make it possible. Her preparation was in
progress. Her call had come, and she said, "Yes."

After five years in San Antonio, my husband was asked to take a
denominational job near Dallas, Texas. We moved to Grand Prairie.
My husband's work required much traveling and material preparation.
At first I helped him write articles, but with Susan in high school, I
turned some of the proofreading and rewriting over to her. By the
time she was taking college correspondence courses, she was also
doing almost full-time writing and editing for her father.

Susan's breathing schedule now permitted her to work all day. On
another check-up trip to Houston, she had been taken off the chest
shell and switched to a positive pressure ventilator, which only
required a small tube blowing air into her mouth and lungs. She could
use this breathing assistance method all day.

In 1969 a woman in our church asked the pastor and missions
committee if they would support her in beginning a mission for
Spanish-speaking people. When they said "Yes," they also offered the
use of a small house the church owned. When Susan and I learned of
it, we asked if we might help. We were welcomed with "open arms."
Susan's commitment was about to be carried out.

Our church friend Jettie had a young Hispanic friend whose
father was continually bringing men up from Mexico to work in his
construction business. (Laws were not as strict in those days.) Jettie
and her friend were anxious that these men hear the gospel while they
were in Texas. So our "mission" was begun. Soon we found the little
house too small. We moved into an old, deserted, rat-infested church
building across town. We had language missions preachers come from

Dallas. But after a neighbor's dog had bitten the organist one Sunday morning, vandals had shot holes in the front door, and we had secured a permanent pastor, we moved into the chapel of our church.

After a short time, we all wanted our "own" building. First Baptist Church agreed, and after a time we had a beautiful, little red brick building over near the far corner of First Baptist Church's parking lot. Susan had already begun teaching children in the old church building. But now she had a nice, big place for her class on Sunday nights. And on Wednesday nights we kept all the children—babies through high school. Even though their parents wanted them taught in English, we sneaked in a few hymns in Spanish. Otherwise, the boys and girls could understand nothing of the worship service. By the time we left, almost all of the children had made a profession of faith and been baptized. The pastor's wife was their Sunday School teacher and shared the credit and joy with Susan.

In 1976 my husband was asked to accept a denominational job in Raleigh, North Carolina. Susan and I were dismayed at the thought of leaving our Hispanic friends, but we knew we had to follow where the Lord led "Daddy." After a time in Raleigh, Susan volunteered to tutor young women who needed to learn English as a second language. She helped three Brazilian women whose husbands were studying at North Carolina State University. In spite of the fact that they spoke Portuguese as their first language, Susan found Spanish to be close enough kin that they had very little difficulty.

Across the road from our church in Raleigh was a big apartment complex where we held a "Big A Club" on Saturdays. There were three boys who lived with their father. Their mother was dead. They came regularly to "Big A Club" and began attending our church, too. Soon all of them had made a profession of faith and been baptized. One of them has maintained contact with us ever since.

After almost ten years in North Carolina, we moved back to Texas for my husband to retire. We moved to Georgetown, near Austin, where our son is a research physicist at the University of Texas. Susan took up her many interests that had developed in Raleigh. Although her income was small, she gave to many "good causes." Our church got the largest part; then came the Hispanic Baptist Theological Seminary in San Antonio. Then there were Friends of the Earth, Habitat for Humanity, American Bible Society, Nature Conservancy, Public Citizen, Baptist World Alliance, United Farm Workers, Salvation Army, Humane Society, American Farmland Trust, Project Vote Smart, and others.

Susan's interests were broad and her involvements, though physically limited, were many by telephone and typewriter. She regularly read the publication from all the "good causes" she contributed to. In addition, she read the monthly science magazine, *Discovery*, *The Biblical Archaeology Review*, and completed ten volumes of the Time-Life Series, *Time Frame*, which covered history from 3000 B.C. to 1300 A.D. (She felt she had pretty well covered the periods after that in her school work.)

Susan also enjoyed her hobbies of drawing, painting, and cross-stitching. She did these with a little frame mounted on the movable desk front built by her father. With her right arm and hand suspended by slings and her pen or brush tied between her fingers, she drew and painted. With her needle clutched between her fingers up against her knuckles, she "sewed."

Six of her "numbered" paintings hang in our den. Two hang in her father's study. Her cross-stitched Christmas ornaments belong to churches where we have been members and to our friends. Her original drawing and cross-stitch of "The Little Train That Could" hangs in the office of Thorkild Engen, director of the Orthotics Department at the Institute for Rehabilitation and Research in Houston. The little train is on top of the hill. It proudly proclaims, "I Thought I Could!"

In our dining room we have Susan's cross-stitched wall hanging with the message, "God bless this house and all who enter here." But in her bedroom hangs her first and most difficult work, "The Serenity Prayer":

> God grant me the serenity to accept the things I cannot change,
> the courage to change the things I can, and the wisdom to know
> the difference.

We believe that these two pieces recorded her values in life. We also believe that she had carried out her "Serenity Prayer." As one prominent minister said, "Susan willed to make a difference."

Another minister said of Susan: "The word 'handicapped' was not in her vocabulary. She faced all of life with courage and faith in God. She was a missionary extraordinaire." And knowing her concern for governmental affairs, he also said, "Susan Ray wrote to more policy makers than any other person I know." Still another denominational worker commented: "She will be remembered for her determination and courage, and her life of service."

Susan stated her own views about her life when she said, "When I think of Helen Keller I think of a great woman who overcame great handicaps. I join others in admiring her for this. But when I think of President Franklin Roosevelt, I think first of a great president of the United States, and second as one with handicaps—polio, in fact. I would prefer to be remembered for what I can contribute rather than for having handicaps."

The last writing assignment Susan had was to help update a text-book on Baptist policy for students in Texas Baptist colleges and universities. She completed and mailed in her assignment just before going to the hospital. But her last cross-stitch work, an American flag, was unfinished. Her crusades were not finished, either. Her roles in getting out missionary information, in beginning and leading a missionary prayer chain, were not finished. Her support for all her "good causes" was not finished.

There was so much more for Susan to do! The pneumonia was under control, her heart rate was coming down, and the doctor had said we could be going home in a couple of days. But Susan said, "I think I'm dying." And I prayed, "Not now, Lord, not now!" But the Lord said, "Now!" The nurses watching her heart monitor said there was one perfect heartbeat, but no next one at all! Susan was placed in the iron lung on February 27, 1952. She was buried on February 27, 1995. For forty-three years she had helped set the pattern of our lifestyle. Now it must be changed radically.

I now hear all kinds of strange sounds at night; they are no longer drowned out by the "whew-whoosh" of the iron lung in the next room. I find it hard to stay home alone when my husband makes short trips to Austin. On longer trips I go with him, something just the two of us have not done in almost forty-seven years.

We experience other changes, also. I must now prepare and present all of the missions programs without Susan's help. We will no longer on Monday morning set up her telephone so Susan can call the Baptist Home and Foreign Mission Boards to get a new prayer request to pass on to the prayer chain captains. We will no longer find her long list of phone numbers in Washington, D.C., or in Austin, Texas, so she can call her senator or representative.

We will no longer set up Susan's word processor and remote keyboard so that she can write letters to editors, TV stations, friends, or magazines, or sometimes write articles—free lance or assignment. My husband must do his own writing, and I must again do all the proofreading. He will have to do all the typing on the word processor because I am unwilling to learn.

We will have to remember to put out the garbage on Tuesday nights. My husband will have to remember to check the smoke alarms regularly and to change the drain fields for the septic tank in January and July. I will have to remember when it is time to start the VCR recording our favorite old comedies on TV in the afternoons. I will also have to remember whether the cats are inside or outside, when their flea collars need changing, what time I put the ham in the oven, and on and on. Susan's brain was always burdened with the mundane affairs of everyday life in order to come to our rescue when we were about to forget.

Because I had to help get Susan ready for Sunday School and begin lunch preparation, I had not been to Sunday School in forty-three years. And before polio struck, I had always worked with children. Now, I am in an adult Sunday School class for the first time in my life.

Perhaps my husband's greatest change is no longer making for Susan all the many things he stayed busy with in his workshop. One of his greatest concerns now is "What to do with all her homemade equipment?" It includes three tank respirators, two reclining chairs, a hydraulic "lift," and five positive-pressure ventilators.

We were able to give away Susan's Olivetti typewriter, which was attached by cable to a small remote keyboard that sat on her clip-on desk (it "clipped on" the arms of her chair). We were also able to give away her Cascade humidifier used with her positive-pressure units.

The only things we wanted to sell were our big Ford van with a swing-out, battery-operated wheelchair lift and our specially "rigged for wheelchair" travel trailer. We sold them together very soon to another family who had need for such equipment.

Yes, our lifestyle is changing, and Susan's work would never have been finished. But the Lord said "Now." We have accepted it, for we know "our times are in His hands." It is not easy, but we know we can lay all our burdens on the Lord, the one who cares for us. And we know we will all be reunited "when we all get to heaven. What a day of rejoicing that will be!"

CHAPTER 9

❧ Our Life after Roger ❧

Ebbie Smith

The telephone's rasping jangle roused us from deep sleep in our home in Kediri, East Java, Indonesia, where we were completing twelve years of missionary service. Lifting the telephone, I heard the voice of our oldest son, Randy, saying, "Dad, come to the hospital quickly; we have had an accident on the highway." Speaking of his fifteen-year-old brother, Roger, he continued, "I don't think Roger is going to make it."

We quickly left word with our dedicated helpers, Wari and Painem, and drove immediately to the Baptist hospital in Kediri. Arriving at the emergency room, we saw Randy, standing beside the gurney with the boys' friend, Yono, and to the side of the room, another gurney with someone covered. Noting the socks protruding from the sheet, we knew this was Roger and that he, as predicted by Randy, had not made it.

I turned to Donna immediately and said, "He is dead." Our doctor friend and fellow missionary, Gene Ruble, turned to us and said with a firm tone, "Yes, he is dead." Donna and I turned to Randy and Yono and attempted to comfort them as Yono continued to receive treatment.

We learned what had happened. Yono and Roger had been on one motor bike, with Randy and another Indonesian friend on the second. They were returning from a performance with Band Egon, the Indonesian band the boys sang with. The performance that night had been in a town about an hour's drive from Kediri. We had thought the boys were going to stay overnight, but Roger had insisted they come home. On the way, a bus refused to relinquish the part of the road rightly occupied by the motor bike with Roger and Yono. The bus struck only the handlebar of the bike, but threw both boys into the side of the bus. Yono was only slightly hurt, but Roger was fatally injured.

Since little emergency equipment is available in that part of Java, Randy was forced to flag a passing taxi to bring Roger, Yono, and himself to the Baptist hospital in Kediri. They arrived around two o'clock in the morning, hence the phone call and our arrival later.

Within minutes, other missionary friends began to arrive at the emergency room. They brought words of comfort and strength. Shortly, I returned to our house to secure burial clothing for Roger. When I told our helpers, Wari and Painem, who had been with us over eleven years, that Roger was dead, Painem sounded the words that I had been thinking: "How will we live without Roger?"

Having done all we could do at the hospital, Donna, Ebb, Randy, Yono (who was released after his injuries were treated), and several other Indonesian friends left the hospital to drive to our home. The sun was just rising over the bamboo and trees. Randy exclaimed, "Look at the beautiful sunrise." These were welcome words, for at that moment, we (Donna's words) needed the assurance that God was still in charge of the world and was still making beautiful sunrises. Arriving at our home, our friends spoke comforting words to our helpers as we placed Yono in Roger's bed.

Another of the boys' Indonesian friends came with the word that the police at the accident scene were demanding that Randy and Yono return to the station. Together with several other friends, I returned with Randy and Yono, telling Donna to try to call our families in the United States. At that time, telephone calls to the United States often took eight to ten hours if they got through at all.

I was gone about two hours. When I returned home, several of our missionary friends had come to our home and were helping to receive the constant line of Indonesian sympathizers. In Javanese culture, the family of a deceased person is never to be left alone for the first several days after the death. Donna was sitting in the living room with about twenty Indonesian men, mostly connected with Egon Band. They did not know what to say. They sat in silence, doing what their culture said should be done on such an occasion. Donna told me she had already talked with my brother in the United States (a miracle call), and he would go to be with my mother. Roger's death came only two months after my father's passing, so I was concerned about her and this second shock.

A few days later, July 4, 1973, we buried Roger in Kediri, right by Ann Ingouf, a twelve-year-old missionary child who had died just

eleven months prior. Few had seen so many people at a funeral in
Indonesia. Randy and Roger were not just well-known, but celebrities
in East Java. They spoke both Indonesian and Javanese as locals.
People had come not just from Kediri, but from other towns as well.
The army officer, for whom the concert had been held on the night of
the accident, brought his entire command. Missionary friends from all
over Indonesia had made difficult trips to be at our sides.

How do you respond to the loss of a child? No parent desires to
bury a child; that is simply not the way it is supposed to happen. How
do we answer Painem's question, "How can we live without Roger?"
May we share a few ideas of how to survive the death of a child?

Accept the reality of death. My statement to Donna, "He is dead,"
and the doctor's immediate and blunt addition, "Yes, he is dead," were
neither cruel nor unnecessary. The fact was stated; the truth of the
event nailed down; the reality accepted. Until one accepts the reality
of death, one will make few advances in the healing process.

Death is never easily received nor readily accepted. We can think
of so many ways it might have been avoided—how greatly we wished
it had not happened. But we must acknowledge without reservation,
"Yes, he is dead." When we know and accept this truth, then healing
can begin.

Refuse to blame God. Those who have lost children to death often
find themselves tempted to blame, or at least question, God. Why did
God allow this precious child to suffer this disease or injury? Why did
God not protect the child from that which took his/her life? Blaming
God brings no child back to life; it only breeds bitterness and resent-
ment in the lives of those who entertain questions about God's care.

We may never understand the ways of life and why God allows
some things to happen. We know that God is in charge of this world.
God's power is not lessened nor the divine ability to protect
diminished. Still, bad things happen—and often to good people. Trust
toward God and continued faith in God's care yields far more benefits
than blaming God or allowing place to bitterness.

In the case of Roger, the friend on the same bike escaped with
only superficial injuries. When Roger fell into the bus, had he fallen
three inches lower, he might well have suffered only a broken

shoulder. As it was, the back bumper of the bus hit his head—slicing a large gash in his protective helmet and inflicting the head wound that resulted in his death. Could God have made him fall three inches lower? Obviously, yes! For some reason, God chose differently.

Perhaps this event spared Roger something far worse that would have happened. At least, we chose not to blame God, but accepted the reality of the accident. So great is the danger of bitterness and blaming God that the apostle Paul wrote, "Get rid of all bitterness, rage and anger, brawling and slander, along with every form of malice" (Eph 4:31 NIV).

Blaming God or others brings no healing, but promotes further suffering and pain. We can only overcome bitterness through the ministry of the Spirit of God. Ask; this peace will be given. Let God free you from the bitterness of blaming Him for life's experiences.

Accept the ministry of others. Love consists of giving to others, sacrificing on behalf of others, living for others. These words express the biblical meaning of love and constitute a truthful statement of how to show love. There is another dimension of love: that of receiving. While it remains true that it is more blessed to give than receive, we must never overlook the truth that receiving ministry and help from others is also an expression of love to them. In a sense, we must love others to really receive comfort, ministry, and help from them.

Roger's death was our first experience of utter helplessness and powerless. When we had lost property to thievery or destruction, it could be replaced. When desires had been thwarted, other opportunities would be forthcoming. But Roger could not, and has not, been replaced. We could not fix our broken hearts or mend the hurt in the other children. We were halfway around the world from Roger's grandparents and other family members. To whom could we turn?

Part of the answer was we could turn to our friends. Missionary friends came from areas far away, traveling by inconvenient means to be with us. One mission executive not only flew to Indonesia, but traveled on the night train to be with us in Kediri. He came to our house, entered without a word, sat in our living room and began to cry. After a few minutes, he ministered to us. Shared burdens do become lighter!

We found comfort and solace from our Indonesian friends as well. One pastor's wife from another city was visiting in Kediri. She came faithfully every day to pray with us and assure us of her interest and God's care. This was a time of tension between missionaries and national convention leaders, but it did not prevent the convention leaders from coming to our sides—to assure us of their love and God's love. Several of these pastors and convention leaders participated in Roger's funeral services.

Members of Band Egon, most of whom were not Christians, agreed to help, but they expresssed some anxiety as they were not familiar with Christian customs relating to funerals. When the time came to move the casket (Indonesian custom is for the casket to be carried by persons close to the deceased), the members of Band Egon forgot their fear and reluctance and performed the Indonesian service—bearing on their shoulders Roger's casket.

An Indonesian member of the Band Egon was a Christian and an employee of the Baptist hospital. We asked him to sing "How Great Thou Art" (the Indonesian translation) at the funeral. He agreed and told others at the hospital, "I am going to go out behind the hospital in the morning and cry by myself until I have cried out, then I will sing that song for Roger without breaking." He did exactly that.

We drew strength from the many expressions of love coming from missionary and national friends. Love allows us to accept such ministry. To the degree we love others, we can allow them to enter our lives and share our sorrows. When tragedy and loss occur, accept the love and ministry of Christian friends. God provides through them for your deepest needs.

Exercise care with siblings. Siblings as well as parents must deal with the death of a family member. Surviving the death of a child may well involve helping the other children in the family deal with the event. We found this need especially intense.

Randy had viewed the accident, brought Roger into town to the Baptist hospital, and dealt immediately with the trauma. His was a long recovery. He needed parents and friends to see him through. Something of Randy's recovery can be seen in that he named his first child, Roger Wayne Smith, in memory of the lost brother.

Robin was especially close to Roger. I realized one day, some weeks after the funeral, how deeply wounded Robin was. I found Robin in his room, looking through his little box of favorite and special things. He looked up at me, pointed to the "things," and said, "Nothing there belonged to Roger!" I realized that while we had given some of Roger's possessions to others, we had really not given anything to Robin. I immediately went to the shelf and took one of Roger's tennis trophies and gave it to Robin. I almost missed a chance to help in Robin's recovery.

With daughter Rianna, the situation was even more involved. Without realizing it, we were making too much of certain facts about Roger's death. The night of the accident, he insisted on returning to Kediri, though the boys had planned to remain overnight in the city where the concert was given. Unknown to Randy, Roger said to several of their friends, "If I get back to Kediri, I will tell you an important secret." He said to others as he was eating, "This is the last banana I will eat." The friends thought nothing of these statements until after the accident.

We talked of these premonitions and wondered if they were that or simply more of Roger's often teasing. Months later, we realized Rianna had extreme fears that she was going to die. Her expression was, "Roger thought he was going to die, and he did. I think I am going to die, and I am afraid I will." Some months passed before this fear subsided.

When death comes to a child in the family, be sensitive to the siblings. Guard against the tendency to make the departed the epitome of all that is good, one to which the other children should aspire. Be certain not to transfer fears to the other children. Affirm each child. Watch for signs of stress, fear, anger, and/or bitterness. Exercise extreme care with siblings of the lost child.

Keep alive remembrances of accomplishments. Remember the sweetness, the special accomplishments, the fun things about the child who died. Roger was special. For weeks after his funeral we continued to receive back from the correspondence high school courses the graded lessons he had finished. They invariably came back with a grade of A. He is remembered as a fine student. When he was in the missionary hostel and American school in Singapore, the teens in the hostel achieved a record of nine A's one semester. Roger was quick to point out that he made six of them.

Roger had quick wit. When one of the missionary mothers who was teaching eighth-grade history gave a test, Roger provided a special answer. The question from the teacher was "Can you name the generals who fought at Gettysburg?" Roger's answer was a terse, "Yes!" The interesting thing is that he was not trying to be a smart aleck. That was his natural, to-the-point, no-nonsense approach.

Roger learned to play tennis very well, earning several trophies while on furlough. When he played boys of his own age, the parents of the other boys declared, "He plays like a man, not like a boy!" We hold these and many other memories of Roger with great delight. Survive the death of a child by keeping alive the memories rather than suppressing them. The memories may at times bring sorrow, but in the long run they will contribute to healing.

Allow the experience to forge you into a better minister. The experience of losing a child can make you a better minister to others. This transformation is not, however, automatic. I tried to share with a man who had lost a son how the loss of Roger had helped us become better ministers to others. This man said solidly, "I don't want to be a minister to others; I just want my boy back!" While understanding his feelings, I grieved for his lost opportunities of reaching out to others.

Donna often says that now we can reach out to others in times of their sorrow and really know how they feel. No one would choose the experience of losing a child just to become a better minister, and many persons become able ministers without such an experience. If circumstances bring you to this loss, the most helpful course is to allow the experience to equip you to reach out to others in times of grief. Every effort at meeting the needs of others in grief situations makes Roger's death a little more meaningful for us.

Few experiences are more blessed than those of touching others in Christian, loving ways. Allow God to use the experience of losing a child to make you a better helper to others. Few avenues are more productive in helping you survive the death of a child.

Refuse to play the "what if" game. Too often when tragedy comes, we are tempted to engage in the age-old game of "what if." What if we had never brought the child to this place? What if circumstances had never led to him being on the highway? What if we had made other decisions about any number of things, then would this death have been averted? These questions naturally arise. Seeking answers to the "what ifs" not only fails to provide answers or helps, but usually these questions prolong grief and lead to further questioning.

No amount of rethinking past decisions or efforts can change what has taken place. We may learn from the experiences, but we cannot alter the circumstances. Allowing the "what if" game to arouse feelings of guilt and remorse helps little or none with the grief-solving process. When the "what ifs" begin to arise—and they will—ask the Lord to sweep them away. Playing the "what if" game provides no genuine help in surviving the death of a child.

Accept the fact that overcoming grief is a process. God forgives immediately upon the repentance of humankind. For humans, however, most spiritual events constitute processes rather than instantaneous experiences. Do not get down on yourself if overcoming your grief takes time. Those who testify that they immediately receive peace in tragedy may not fully remember their experiences. Allow yourself some time to fully accept and implement God's gift of peace.

You should feel no guilt if you need significant time to come to peace with your grief. The hurt may never fully go away. In time, God's grace will complete the process, and you will find peace and victory. Give yourself this space.

These words are not meant to say that in time you will forget the hurt of loss. It is to say that in time God will work in your life to give you the grace to accept the situation and continue to function in God's will. Do not compare your recovery with others. The process of overcoming grief requires different methods and longer periods for some. Such needs do not mean less faith or weaker spiritual resources. Accept the grief process; expect some setbacks. Another way to survive the death of a child relates to accepting the way to peace in grief situations as a process and giving yourself time to understand and accept God's working.

Depend fully on God. The fullest victory over the trauma of losing a child cannot be secured by human action or effort. This kind of hurt can only be assuaged by the power of God who gave the child. You are broken and crushed and powerless. But God knows and cares. This is the place "at the farthest limits of the sea" at which you have arrived only to find the Lord there before you to make possible the impossible experience (see Ps 139:9-10). The promise, "I am with you always, to the end of the age" remains certain (Matt 28:19-20). Final victory in the experience of losing a child comes only through the Lord's care.

The loss of a child often represents the darkest of parental experience. In this night there seems only darkness—no light. But God in divine mercy can bring light and recovery. Rely on God, and peace can come. With the psalmist, the wounded parent can say, "By day the Lord commands his steadfast love, and at night his song is with me, a prayer to the God of my life" (42:8).

CHAPTER 10

❧ A Tribute to Don ❧

Jack U. Harwell

At its very best, life is often extremely difficult. At its very worst, life is often unfair. Both of these axioms came true in the abbreviated life of my late son, Donald Ray Harwell. Don was born on October 25, 1955, just six minutes after his twin brother, Ronald Horace Harwell. Don died of AIDS complications on July 1, 1994.

I am a journalist and have been since 1950. But I cannot find the words to express how deeply I loved Don, nor how profoundly he is missed now that he is gone. Not an hour goes by that I don't long to call him up to arrange a golf game, to talk about hot-button political issues, to lament the latest theological skirmishes, or to just check on how he is getting along. But that is impossible now. Don is no more except a legacy, a buried treasure, a shining memory of thirty-nine years of joy and accomplishment and talent and kindness that now adorns the hallowed halls of heaven.

Many emotions surge through a grieving father as he tries to summarize what it means to lose a child so young. I long to bring back precious moments of sharing and love. I hunger to undo hurts and slights I wish I had never allowed to happen. I covet from the depths of my soul more time to talk over the many ideas and philosophies and plans and dreams we shared during Don's thirty-nine-year pilgrimage among us.

But the greatest pain of all is knowing that the whole world will not get to know Don as we knew him. He had so much to offer, and he was so willing to share it. I find it hard to ever imagine agreeing that it was "fair" for Don to go without the world benefitting from his mind, talents, and spirit. It is not "fair" that Don never got to own a home, find a mate for life, sire a child, and know the fulfillment of seeing his talents and commitments bring forth fruit in a fulfilled life.

Many times when I think of Don, I try to envision my first moments upon arrival in heaven. After I hug and kiss Don a few thousand times, I am going to ask our Heavenly Father why He allowed Don to go so early. Not being a theologian, I cannot imagine what God will answer. But being a father, I can believe He would say something like: "I understand your feelings totally. My son was only 33 when he died; that was 2,000 years ago, and all the world still does not know what he had to offer. I understand and I care. Now enjoy Don for the aeons of time. He's yours forever because he's mine, too."

For now, the most redemptive thing I have found to do in honor of Don's memory is to love Ron even more than I did before—if that is possible. This article could well be about Ron. He was such a faithful brother for Don throughout Don's years of health and sickness. Ron neglected his own marvelous wife, Lisa, and their three children to minister to Don through eight long years of HIV and AIDS-related decline. Ron is rebuilding relationships with his wife and children, which suffered because of his devotion to Don and his myriad needs. And Ron is exhibiting the same kindness, patience, and wisdom in that journey as he demonstrated in his limitless care for Don. Again, I cannot find the words to say how proud I am of Ron, and of Lisa, Kelly, Andrew, and Terri.

But this article is not about Ron. It is about Don. So let me tell you something about Don's life so you will know why all who knew him well believe his going left such a large hole in so many hearts in Georgia and Tennessee. I admit to prejudice; maybe after reading this piece, you will understand some of my fatherly pride.

During his growing-up years, Don was a brilliant student. He made straight A's at every level of elementary and high school and most of fifteen years of college. He was president of his student body in high school, was voted the most outstanding senior, played the piano and trumpet, played on the high school golf team, and was active in secular politics. (We had the only Andrew Young political signs in our all-white neighborhood in the 1960s, when that was not the "safe" thing to do. But Don did it anyway.) Don and Ron were probably the only students in their school to vote for George McGovern for President. They campaigned hard for Jimmy Carter and Walter Mondale, and Don went to their inauguration in Washington.

This fervent commitment to political and social causes made Don feel he wanted to become a history teacher. He entered Georgia State University in Atlanta with that singular goal in mind. He worked full-time at Georgia Baptist Medical Center for five years while earning his full college costs. He then entered Vanderbilt University in Nashville to seek a master's degree and a doctorate in history. He got his master's degree in quick order and taught history at Vanderbilt for two more years, working toward his doctorate.

During those four years, Don worked part-time and full-time at Parkview Hospital in Nashville. He also got deeply involved in the music ministry of West End United Methodist Church, just across the street from Vanderbilt. He made a decision to become a Methodist and remained such until his death. At his request, Don was cremated and his ashes are now in the columbarium at West End United Methodist Church.

But Don did not do as well on his doctoral exams as he wished— the first time in his life Don had not been the best at anything he tried—and he began to re-examine his career plans. He returned to Atlanta, enrolled at Georgia State again, went to work at Piedmont Hospital, and obtained a master's degree in business, then another master's degree in hospital administration. By this time, Don had almost fifteen years experience in hospital administration, and he knew what he wanted do for the rest of his life.

Upon getting that third master's degree, Don was employed as assistant administrator of Hutcheson Medical Center in Fort Oglethorpe, Georgia, just across the state line from Chattanooga, Tennessee. I have never seen Don so happy as he was for those three years in Fort Oglethorpe. He jumped into hospital administration with both feet. He joined civic clubs, volunteered for a local hospice program, and worked in an AIDS ministry. He joined a Methodist church choir. He played golf with his boss, his minister, and his father or brother when time and finances allowed. Life looked rosy for Don. His family and friends were thrilled for him.

Let me say at this point that there was never any doubt about Don's Christian faith or his mature understandings of Christianity during those fifteen years of college. When he was only about nineteen years-old, Don wrote a term paper entitled "Christian Symbolism in John Steinbeck's *Grapes of Wrath*." It was one of the finest sermonic pieces I have read anywhere; I treasure it in my files to this day. While working on his doctorate in history at Vanderbilt, Don wrote a marvelous research paper on the role of Christian chaplains during the War Between the States. Again, it was careful, mature, positive, and full of faith and hope . . . and scholarship. It was worthy of any seminary student in the land!

While still an early teenager, Don was thrown out of his Sunday School class one day because he challenged the teacher's telling of racist jokes to young boys. His spiritual idol, a pastor who shared Don's theological and political and social views ardently, was fired from our church pulpit about that time, allegedly for his open views on race and women's rights. Don never fully recovered from that spiritual blow.

Every discussion Don and I had about religious faith—and they were many and they were often heated—was engaged because Don cared. Don knew his Savior, and he was proud to be an intelligent, articulate—and sometimes acerbic—critic of those who didn't see the larger dimensions of the Christian faith being lived out in the flesh-and-blood world of health care, political realities, racial justice, theological integrity, and AIDS.

How Don did love Jimmy and Rosalyn Carter! From his days as a high school student, volunteering to work in the "Peanut Brigade," Don had a strong appreciation for Carter's intellectual honesty, political vision, human-rights compassion, and pragmatic religion. While still a graduate student at Vanderbilt, Don wrote an article about how he thought future historians would view Jimmy Carter's presidency. The article was printed with major headlines in the *Atlanta Journal-Constitution*. The editorial page editor called Don on the phone and told him he could write for his newspaper any time he desired. But sadly, soon after that Don learned he had an incurable illness, and he turned his editorial skills toward becoming an AIDS activist.

But that's getting a little ahead of the narrative trail of Don's life. In 1987, just after Don had gotten his coveted position at the hospital in Fort Oglethorpe, he learned he was HIV positive. At first, he didn't tell his family. He was so fiercely independent and so determined to find some way to lick the problem. But eventually he told his beloved twin brother, Ron, and asked Ron to tell me. Ron and I both cried on each other's shoulders. A week later, at Don's request, we told his mother. She was even more distraught.

A marriage that had been in difficulty for a long time was about to face severe strains, and an eventual breakup. The contrasting ways in which his mother and I reacted to Don's illness sharply dramatized the differences in our basic approaches to life. Those differences ultimately led to our divorce in 1991. It was a major tragedy that the divorce happened as Don approached his death, and he spent many months feeling that his illness was somehow responsible for our divorce. Before Don died, he wrote that he knew the divorce was in process long before he got sick. I thank God Don knew that for certain before he died.

For three years, Don was able to continue working despite his HIV infections. He had several sick spells, and he and I and his brother Ron spent thousands of dollars on HIV medications. Having to keep his HIV status secret meant he could make no insurance claims. But in the spring of 1990, what Don called "my worst nightmare" actually happened. He was involved in an automobile accident, just a few blocks from the hospital where he worked. He was severely injured and was bleeding profusely. Don had enough awareness and integrity that he told the emergency medical technicians, ambulance drivers, and nurses he was HIV positive and they should not touch his blood. Now, his secret was out.

Soon, he was diagnosed as having full-blown AIDS. Soon after that, he was out of a job. But God provided for awhile. Don had been a faithful volunteer in an organization called Chattanooga CARES (Council on AIDS Research, Education, and Service). Two months after losing his job at the hospital, he was asked to become executive director of Chattanooga CARES. Don held this position for more than two years, until he became too disabled to work.

Volumes could be written about the people who ministered to Don during those last four years of his life, and about the people to whom Don ministered. I know I'm a bragging father, but I honestly believe Don was the catalyst for making Chattanooga CARES one of the most respected AIDS service groups in the Southeast. He went all over Tennessee and Georgia, speaking and counseling and writing and organizing on behalf of AIDS sufferers and their families. His CARES group in Chattanooga won many awards for its creative and aggressive ministry to people with AIDS and their loved ones. Don was the persistent stackpole around which that ministry prospered for two years.

Don wrote a regular column for the Chattanooga CARES newsletter. It was a series of essays on what it means to live with AIDS. The largest AIDS organization in Atlanta read Don's columns and asked him to write for them, too. After he was forced to go on disability in 1992, Don was asked to continue writing the columns. As death became imminent, he spent his last lucid months selecting and editing those essays into manuscript form. He made Ron promise to "get my book published after I'm gone."

Don's only motives were to alert more people to the realities of this ravaging disease, and to help AIDS sufferers know more about how to cope with the daily horrors of their declining days. And those horrors are gruesome. Neither space nor decorum allow me to delineate the many miseries and indignities Don suffered through more than seven years of HIV/AIDS sickness and treatment.

The physical devastation was grim: loss of weight, hacking coughs, vomiting spells, severe asthma, hepatitis, lung problems, gall bladder surgery, debilitating cramps, pain in every joint, insomnia, and so on and so on. We lost count of the number of hospital stays, major surgeries, mountains of pills, and all-night agonies. My heart would almost break in the agony of seeing Don suffer so, and not being able to do anything tangible to relieve his misery.

But the worst pain of all was to see his mental and emotional reactions to some of the medications he received. Don called them "psychotic episodes." They were usually caused by prednisone. Don would be completely irrational for days at a time. He would have horrible hallucinations—the FBI was after him, the CIA was about to get him, Ronald Reagan was trying to trap him, George Bush had assigned agents to silence him . . . on and on his imagination would race in groundless disarray. And at times he would get on weird, psychotic, spiritual trails . . . making signs of the cross all over the house; calling out to gods and spirits he imagined to be in every corner of his room; "lining up" with his hands all of the spiritual forces of the universe to focus on his body and his illness. Those were the worst times of all, knowing what a magnificent mind Don R. Harwell really possessed, and seeing what medication and disease could do to confuse and detour that glorious brain of his.

Many times we had to go into another room so Don wouldn't see us crying out of fear and pain and frustration at our inability to understand or to help him through these episodes. The only cure seemed to be to take him "cold turkey" off the offending medications, which would then restart some severe physical problem. It was a vicious cycle. I must confess: The only times in my life I ever came close to doubting the mercy and justice of an omnipotent Heavenly Father was when I saw Don in those psychotic episodes. I developed a keen appreciation for what I had read from an un-remembered author many years ago: "The closest I ever came to doubting the existence of God was when I saw patients in a mental ward of a psychiatric hospital."

One positive emotion that grew out of these psychotic episodes was the deep relationship that developed between Don and my second wife, Teliea, whom I married in May of 1992. Teliea is an ordained minister who has special training in pastoral care. She is a loving and tender woman who seemed to find ways to relate to Don that others could not find. Without slighting what any other caregiver did for Don in his last months, I believe Teliea was a "special" caregiver for whom Don had a special bond. This has made me love Teliea even more. She was not Don's natural mother, but she couldn't have been a more loving and devoted caregiver through his final days. Don's beloved "Aunt Nan"—my only sister, Eleanor Anne Harwell—also ministered to Don mightily. So did his mother. Aunt Nan was with Don when he died on July 1, 1994, at 1:00 A.M.

May I confess something else? I did not do enough to let Don know that I was proud of him and grateful for him and thankful to God for letting Ron and Don be my sons. To my grave, I will carry a nagging regret that I should have done more to assure Don of the abiding pride I had for his life and his integrity and his Christian grace, even through the ravages of AIDS. Because I was editor of Baptist newspapers most of my adult life, Don thought I was afraid his illness would be a political liability to me, and that I tried to cover up the fact of his AIDS condition. This was not true; but I should have been more aggressive in countering that feeling in Don's mind.

Just a few months before Don died, I wrote "An Open Letter to My Son, Don," in *Baptists Today,* for which I have been editor since June, 1988. I bared my soul to my readers, and to any others who might see the column, in telling Don how proud I was of him and how thankful I was that God had given him to us for 39 years.

I had several motives in writing that column. One was to somehow let a few more Baptists be aware that AIDS is not going away, and that even a well-known Christian editor can experience AIDS in his own family. But my major purpose in writing the column was for Don—to let him see his Dad going on public record as acknowledging his AIDS and voicing his love for and faith in his dying son. I truly believe the column accomplished both purposes. I know I saw Don smile a smile I will treasure until my dying day when Teliea read the column to him in May of 1994, just six weeks before he died. I wish now I had written it three years earlier.

Indirectly, that column in *Baptists Today* has helped me and Teliea to find a special way to try to adjust to Don's homegoing. Because it appeared in a national Baptist publication, and has been reprinted in several other papers and books, we have been invited to several churches and religious groups to talk about churches and their ministry to AIDS sufferers. We have been able to tell Don's story to Christians who have AIDS in their family circles or who want to understand AIDS better so they can minister to AIDS sufferers and their families in their towns. I believe Teliea and I are extending Don's life and passion for AIDS ministry when we make these appearances. I know it helps us.

Personally, I have also been helped by reading several books dealing with grief and loss and death. Teliea has bought several for me; she alone knows how much I lie awake at night thinking of Don, or ride down southern highways talking about Don, or sit on airplanes reminiscing about special memories of Don. Outside of the Holy Bible, the one book that has helped me the most was written by my treasured friend, Hardy Clemons. The book is entitled, *Saying Goodbye to Your Grief* (Smyth & Helwys). I was so helped by Hardy's book that I wrote a column about it, which was also therapeutic. For some people, talking their problems out is redemptive. For me, writing about them is my best therapy. I seem to talk better with my fingers than with my mouth.

I mentioned earlier Don's desire to have "my book" published. Ron and I fulfilled our promise to Don. The book was published in May of 1995, under the title Don chose: *Shadowboxing the Grim Reaper—50 Essays from the Front Lines of AIDS.* It is now distributed to AIDS ministry groups across the country as an effort to share the honest and positive story of one young man who struggled and died with AIDS, but who never lost a single battle with his mind and spirit and eternal soul. I believe Ron and Teliea and I—and many others in the widening circle of Don's family and friends—are adding to Don's legacy and honoring his memory by distributing his intelligent-but-humble message to many AIDS sufferers and their caregivers.

As was typical of Don's style, he planned his funeral service in meticulous detail—every song, prayer, scripture verse, and eulogy speaker. And Don took the unusual step of having "A Farewell Message" printed on the program for his funeral service. I can think of no more fitting way to conclude this testimony to a noble son than to quote in full Don's "Farewell Message":

A Farewell Message

I realize that is unusual to pen one's own farewell message and to plan one's own memorial service. But those of you who know me well also know that I always try to have the last word. Thank you for humoring me one final time. As I look back on my life, my failures have been numerous and spectacular: my college vocal audition, my doctoral exams, a lifelong inability to control tongue and temper, hubris, and a string of broken relationships, both personal and familial. And now my most spectacular failure of all—to live a long life.

Yet it is not these disappointments upon which my vision is now focused. Indeed, each served as a valuable learning experience, turning points in my journey. My piano teacher once said, "Your only problem is that you tackle pieces that are too difficult for you." Surely she was right, and not just about the piano. For in the end, life itself proved too difficult for me. The hopeless romantic in a most unromantic time. Perhaps the best that can be said is that I kept trying.

Rather it is joy, gratitude, and satisfaction which I most feel as I look back over the years. It has been my good fortune to live in three of the finest cities in the country during the most dynamic era in human history. I was privileged to have studied and taught in two excellent universities, inspired by caring mentors and eager, inquiring students. I count myself fortunate to have served in four different institutions of healing, where love and concern for patients and their families were the guiding principles. And I was honored by the opportunity to play a small role on the front lines, fighting against the most formidable disease and the greatest social challenge of our time.

I wish to express my profound thanks to the many loving friends and family members who stood beside me in my battle with AIDS, and even to those who did not. No one could enjoy a more golden circle of love and support. Allow me to acknowledge the wisdom of several ministers from a variety of faiths who served as anchors and guides along my circuitous faith journey. The wrong turns along the way I made all by myself. A great debt is also owed to my physicians and nurses who patiently and kindly guided me through the mine fields of AIDS for longer than anyone had a right to hope for.

More prosaic pleasures and opportunities have been allowed me as well. Traveling with friends to sing and worship in the capitals and cathedrals of Europe, marching on the White House, exploring the exotic volcanoes of Hawaii, skiing in the Rockies, snorkeling the crystal waters of the Caribbean, and journeying to the Pacific Northwest are adventures enjoyed by few in a lifetime. Witnessing a presidential inauguration, marveling at the treasures of King Tutankhamen and the British Crown Jewels, and communing with Thomas Jefferson at Monticello were unforgettable thrills as well. And I would be remiss not to recall breaking 80 on the golf course, cheering the Atlanta Braves twice in the World Series, and being present as Hank Aaron rounded the bases for the 715th time to become the greatest slugger of all time.

Certainly no one wants to die young, and I would be dishonest not to lament the future I will not live to see, a future which holds my nieces and nephew growing into adulthood, racial harmony, a cure for AIDS, and a day when men and women are not condemned and ostracized solely on the basis of whom they love.

Yet, like Abraham Lincoln's legs which were just long enough to reach the ground, I have lived just long enough—long enough to discover the magic of Maya Angelou and the music of Aaron Copland and Randall Thompson; to rediscover the wit and wisdom of Mark Twain and Charles Dickens; to experience the majesty of Verdi and Puccini and draw from the strength of personal heroes as diverse as Katherine Hepburn, Ryan White, Dale Murphy, Jimmy Carter, and Martin Luther King Jr. Long enough to learn the joy of children, to worship, to accept love and help from others, and to question long-held assumptions.

Thus, do not weep for me. The pages of history and the daily newspapers are full of many stories far more tragic and lives cut considerably shorter than my own. And know that I die without malice, without self-pity, and with but few regrets. Indeed, I feel oddly like one of the luckiest persons who ever lived.

Farewell and God bless.

* * * * *

Farewell, Don. Yes, God did bless all of us when God gave us you, even if just for thirty-nine years. You made the world a better place in which to live and serve our Savior. In our minds and hearts, we will have you for eternity. Thank you, Lord!

CONTRIBUTORS

Walt and Elizabeth Barnes live in Raleigh, North Carolina, where Walt supervises a soil analysis laboratory and Elizabeth does technical writing for a software development company. They are the parents of Chip, a Navy aviation officer; Elizabeth, also a writer; and Janet, who died in 1988 at age nine.

Caralie Nelson Brown is a retired high school teacher who lives in Raleigh, North Carolina. She is the mother of three children: Nancye Gaj, Anne Kelly, and Raymond Bryan Brown, Jr., the subject of "The Gift of Bryan." She spends many happy hours with her grandchildren: Caran, Carter, Jennifer, and Paul.

Tony W. Cartledge has written for a variety of academic and professional publications. He and his wife, Jan, are ministers at a church near Raleigh, North Carolina. They are the parents of Russ, now in college, and of Bethany, whose untimely death at age seven is recorded in this book.

Lue Ann Claypool, who relates the story of the death of her young daughter, Laura Lue, lives in Fort Worth, Texas, where she works for an oil and gas company. She is also active in the cultural life of the city. Her greatest joy is visiting her son, Rowan, and his family in Louisville, Kentucky, where she is known as "Nana" and has an easy touch for reading "one more story."

Jack U. Harwell, who shares a tribute to his deceased adult son, Don, has been a religious journalist since 1957, having worked in secular journalism prior to then. He has been very active in community and denominational concerns and organizations. He has one living son, Ron, and three grandchildren. He and his wife, Teliea, live in Atlanta, Georgia.

Richard S. Hipps is a pastor in Greensboro, North Carolina, following ten years of missionary service in South America. He and his wife, Patricia, have two children, Justin and Lacey. Their daughter, Alexandria, died in 1993 at the age of four.

Julian S. Orrell is a retired minister and has served in overseas partnership missions. He and his wife, Eleanor, have three children and four grandchildren. In this book he tells of the tragic deaths of his grandson and son-in-law.

Charlene Andrews Ray and her husband, Cecil, of Texas are the parents of Lanny and the grandparents of Jennifer Leigh and Michael Wayne. Their adult daughter, Susan, a respiratory polio quadriplegic, is deceased.

Ebbie C. Smith is a seminary professor. He and wife, Donna, are former missionaries to Indonesia. They have three children: Randy, Robin, and Rianna. Their teenage son, Roger, was killed in Java and is buried there.

Harold N. West, Jr. is a pastor in South Carolina. He and his wife, Elliott, have a daughter, Laura, and a son, Brian. Their young son, Philip, died in 1985.